BOO

pilot

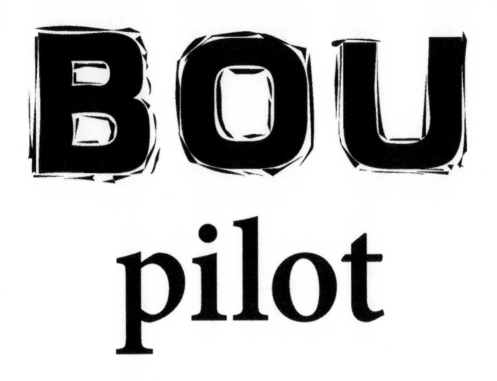

BOU
pilot

JON DRURY

REDEMPTION
PRESS

Published by Redemption Press, PO Box 427, Enumclaw, WA 98022

Toll Free (844) 2REDEEM (273-3336)

Redemption Press is honored to present this title in partnership with the author. The views expressed or implied in this work are those of the author. Redemption Press provides our imprint seal representing design excellence, creative content, and high quality production.

ISBN 13: 978-1-68314-525-7 (Paperback)
978-1-68314-526-4 (ePub)
978-1-68314-527-1 (Mobi)

Library of Congress Catalog Card Number: 2017957329

Jon and Clyde Wilson in An Khe, Vietnam, spring 1969

Thanks

Over the five plus years of this project, many have played a role in completing *BOU Pilot*. The first editors to read all or parts of the manuscript were Dianne Smith and Karen O'Connor. Great input came from Castro Valley Christian Writers and Hayward Writers, led in turn by Kari West, Diane Smith, and Carol Hall. More current help came from Vancouver Christian Writers.

A different input came from Linda Stirling and the Southwest Washington/Oregon Write to Publish group that gave invaluable input on fiction and story technique. They made many of the stories come alive and better connect with the reader.

Editing in the final stage came from Joyce Erickson and from Ron Lester of the Caribou Association.

My insightful first reader has usually been my wife, Beverly, with her loving red pen.

Note that editorial styles differ. Many military manuscripts have aircraft names and call-signs in italics. The manuscript currently follows the *Chicago Manual of Style*.

FOREWORD

Jon tells about his experiences flying the C-7A Caribou in Vietnam right after receiving his Air Force wings. Each vignette is a two-page account in the air or on the ground during his Vietnam tour in 1968 to1969. Each tale is captivating and written so that both military and civilian readers can appreciate what it was like for a young Second Lieutenant to cope with flying combat missions in situations. He and his squadron mates were expected to do the hazardous and challenging job while maintaining peacetime performance, e.g. accidents per flying hour, on-time takeoffs, missions flown.

During the Vietnam War, forty Caribou personnel lost their lives while doing the tactical airlift missions assigned to the 483rd Tactical Airlift Wing. Some of these Air Force personnel were his friends, so telling these tales was not easy for him. I know how that feels because I was a C-7A pilot flying the Caribou in Vietnam during the same timeframe.

Jon's style of writing grabs the reader, holds their interest, and makes them want to read more about the deeds of warriors called upon to fight a long, cruel, and frustrating war. The conflict ended without achieving freedom and independence for the people of South Vietnam. That is a sad result for the veterans who gave so much while serving their country.

Reading the stories brings out his flying skills, human compassion, and faith to a degree one might not expect from a warrior. These elements reflect the skills, passion, determination, and generosity of a man sent to war who found a deeper meaning inside himself than he anticipated.

"Well done, thou good and faithful servant" (Matt. 25:21). You did good then, later in life, and still do that today. Thanks for being who you are—a fellow aviator, a friend, and one who walks in the footsteps of Jesus.

E. Patrick Hanavan, Jr. Ph.D.
Colonel, USAF (Ret.)
Instructor Pilot, 535th Tactical Airlift Squadron, Vung Tau, RVN
Chief Test Pilot, 483rd Tactical Airlift Wing, Cam Ranh Bay, RVN

PREFACE

Why would a lowly transport pilot write a book? What could there be to tell?

"I picked up my load, kicked the tires, lit the fires (started my engines), and took my load where they told me. THE END."

No dogfights with the Red Baron. No enemy shot down. No ordinance (bombs) dropped. How boring!

Some may be surprised that a transport pilot would write a memoir. Surely, the more stirring accounts of warfare are written by fighter pilots or the infantry. But, as a veteran reader of US military accounts, in all conflicts, I immensely enjoy the detailed accounts of those who served—even the routine. Someone has said that aviation is hours of boredom interspersed with moments of stark terror. So is military service for everyone in a combat zone.

Memoirs create archives, but they also help us learn from history. Military action in combat illustrates teamwork in a big task, often at great sacrifice. For many, reading about courage in the challenges of combat inspires courage in present living.

The rescuers in our society are many. First responders such as police, fire fighters, and medical technicians risk their lives. Military personnel are also rescuers, willing to give their lives to defend our freedoms and, on occasion, the freedom of others.

A friend once said, "Every man's account of the details of his life tells a story. That account could fill multiple volumes."

I have never forgotten my friend's words. When I study the story of others, I am a broader, richer, and better person.

Here, forty plus years after the events, I am well aware of the frailty of memory. Though I have suitcases full of fight manuals and records, I do not profess to have remembered things accurately. I yield to the one who says, "It didn't happen that way!" Changes have been made due to invaluable input from others. Instead of professing that everything in these accounts is true, I can only say I have recorded my memory of these events. In places, I have supplied details to make the story I recall more vivid for the reader.

I have tried to limit any accounts that would embarrass or indict anyone, and, when I have included them, names are not used.

In the process of another writing project in the spring of 2012, I realized I was forgetting the details of my service: 1968–1969 in Vietnam. I set the other project aside to record my memories for my family or others interested.

I have written the stories as short-read chapters of 350–450 words because the length is a convenient one to tell one incident I remember.

My story is the account of one person with a routine assignment. Though only one person's story is the weakness of this account, it is also its strength. I was there.

TABLE OF CONTENTS

TO FLY

THE HEAVENS
AND THE EARTH

The explosion rocked my lazy summer morning, and I could see the boiling tower of flame and smoke a mile away. Sirens shrieked and a friend hollered, "A plane crashed down on Hesperian Boulevard!"

I had to get there to see it. I yelled, "Mom, I am going down to see the plane crash," then ran the ten blocks to the accident site in San Lorenzo, California. The explosion had blown pieces of the yellow fabric skin of the airplane everywhere. At first, the hoses of the firemen from three hook-and-ladder trucks, lights flashing, did little to reduce the fierce blaze.

I found a guy in a tan overcoat who looked like my dad and tugged on his sleeve.

"Hey, Mister, what happened?" I hollered over the tumult.

"Two guys stole a plane from the Hayward Airport over there," he yelled back above the din. "They tried to do a loop where the airplane goes all the way over." He motioned in a circle with his hand. "They didn't have enough altitude. They clipped that warehouse and crashed into that mobile home. Luckily nobody was in there," he explained. Piles of clothes burned around the shell of the rounded aluminum mobile home.

How could they steal it, I puzzled? "Don't they haf'ta have a key or something? My dad's Kaiser has to have a key," I asked.

"I don't know kid. Ask that guy in the blue shirt. He works at the airport."

I continued my quest, "Hey, Mister, how could they steal the airplane? Doesn't it have to have a key?"

"No, kid. An old plane like that Piper Cub just needs someone to turn on the ignition switch and someone to turn the propeller. If she kicks over and has gas, off you go into the wild blue yonder."

After perhaps an hour, most of the fire quenched, I was jarred by the firemen emerging with two charred corpses on stretchers. *Wow! They really died.*

Why would they steal it? I wondered. *Did they just want a free joy ride? Big price to pay.*

I saved a piece of the yellow skin. The coolest thing ever. Don't have it any more, so I guess my mom threw it out.

The incident made a big impression on me. I had never flown in an airplane, but it sounded wonderful. It had to be a high, fresh world, a realm apart from the tract houses, dirt, and lawn of my everyday existence. Instead of deterring me, the crash awoke in me a sense of the mystery of flight.

Another yellow airplane, this time a model, would inspire my urge to fly.

DESIRE TO SOAR

The model JN-4 "Jenny" World War I trainer[1] hung above my dad, Howard's, desk in my school days in resplendent yellow enamel. With its guy wires, and red, white, and blue Army Air Corps markings, the plane symbolized my dad's love for flying.

An eight-year-old when World War I began, my dad idolized aviation headliners such as Eddie Rickenbacker and the Hat in the Ring Squadron, Americans Dad considered to be singlehandedly winning the Great War. In faded overalls, at his farm in Early, Iowa, he reveled in every scrap of news he could glean. He was *there* in spirit with the men, freed from tiresome farm chores. He wanted to fly, too.

Every plane he saw stoked the fire. But money for flying lessons was scarce on an Iowa farm. His brother Cliff developed a method of sneaking a few farm chickens, never accurately counted, hiding them in a gully, and then selling them in town. Whether my dad used the same ruse to raise cash, I don't know. But he finally had enough for his first lesson in a tan JN-4 biplane, instructed by a barnstormer. He loved it all—the cough and smell of the engine, the responsiveness of the controls, the freedom from the earth. But life moved on to college, marriage to my mom, and a relocation to the West Coast without completing his pilot's license.

While raising our young family, Dad battled unemployment. Our Spartan lifestyle left no money for additional flying lessons. But my parents still experienced joy as young marrieds, growing a young family in ticky-tacky World War II veteran's housing. My father taught in the local junior high school. During breaks from reading, writing, and 'rithmetic, he oozed the principles of flight. As a preschooler, I gushed with pride over my dad the teacher. Pictures of airplanes and other aviation displays crowded his small Quonset-hut classroom. The students loved it. Always a patriot, he championed the role of aviation in our nation's history.

Dad was my staunchest cheerleader when the Air Force sent me to pilot training. By that time, he was a double-leg amputee due to a three-pack-a-day smoking habit from his teens after his mother had died in giving birth to him and his twin. Sadly, by then he was also in a state mental hospital. But he kept a coffee-table book on the history of the Air Force in his wheel chair. Buttons bursting, he told everyone about his amazing son.

Dad's love of aviation lit the spark that moved me to fly. Though confined to a wheelchair, my dad still soared in the clouds, fulfilling his dreams through me.

THE DRAFT

ollege campuses exploded in protests, tear gas swirled, and conscientious objectors and other anti-war protestors burned their draft cards. In the early '60s, the nation activated the draft due to the buildup for the Vietnam War. The University of California at Berkeley emerged as a hotbed of protest.

Their anger puzzled me. My father had served as a lieutenant in World War II, and his military service fascinated me. In the crawl space under our family home, I found my dad's Army duffel bag. The treasure inside held a life I did not know but was evidenced by brown, wrinkled uniforms, hats, insignia, and medals. My dad had served, and I was immensely proud of that.

Not far from Berkeley, in Hayward, California, I registered with most other eighteen-year-olds and got my draft card, classified 1A. The draft office seemed to exist peacefully next door to Chicken Delight where I worked for a time accumulating moving violations as a delivery car driver.

One night, objectors broke into the draft office and lodged their protest by pouring blood over the draft records. *Is that the best way to make your point?* I wondered.

Following graduation from California State University, I walked into an Air Force recruiting office in Oakland and applied for Officer Training School (OTS). I wanted to fly! By then I had the requisite bachelor's degree, so the application process proceeded smoothly. The next stop was Travis Air Force Base (AFB) in Fairfield, California where I tested for admission to officer and flying training. I qualified for both based on tests that included spatial perception, hearing, and sight.

What didn't qualify was my teeth. "Son, your teeth look like Swiss cheese," the Air Force dentist noted. My family had always been too broke to afford costly dental procedures. The extensive work had to be done in successive appointments.

Strangely enough, the draft process and the application for the Air Force continued side-by-side. In February 1966, I received my draft notice. I had either to meet my induction or show I was in process for another military position. Then the Air Force declared they owned me.

I assumed being qualified for flight meant that I would automatically be given a slot for pilot training. Though accepted for Officer Training School (OTS), my post-graduation assignment to Missile Launch Officer training shocked me! This prospect was about as appealing as cleaning up after a horse parade. I had tested for pilot and had passed the tests. I wanted to fly. Someone suggested I write to the OTS commander and request a Pilot Training opening. I did, and I got it. In July 1966, I would head for Lackland AFB, Texas, for the first step in training.

First Time Up

"How much flying experience have you had?"

The question I expected when applying for Air Force pilot training in the spring of 1966 never came. Later I would learn why. The Air Force wanted men with zero flying experience so there'd be nothing to unlearn.

Growing up during the Korean War, I loved the pictures of fighter jets in the air war. I littered my school papers with drawings of F-86s, the hottest jet prominent in that conflict. School subjects other than airplanes bored me.

My family never flew. The short car trips we took were never more than fifty miles from home. We had no money to fly. I felt fortunate if I could ride the bus. When I walked, I plugged the holes in my shoes with cereal box tops.

But once accepted for pilot training, I longed to give flying a try. A coupon in the newspaper offered a five-dollar sample training flight at the Oakland Airport. Wearing my dad's World War II Army coat, I headed to the airport, coupon in hand.

Built in 1927 and dedicated by Charles A. Lindberg himself, the Oakland Airport had expanded over the years to international status. But when I walked through the door of the flight school on the older side of the field, no one was there. No pilots, students, or instructors. Flying magazines littered a coffee table. The worn brown leather sofa and the faint odor of stale perspiration spelled a favorite spot to flop and snooze.

"Anybody here?" I hollered.

A middle-aged man with a leather face and jacket appeared, and I produced my coupon. His disappointed frown said he was looking for new, *paying* students, not a freeloader with a coupon to waste his time and aviation fuel.

Despite his disdain, he locked the doors, grabbed two headsets, and walked me out to a low-wing Piper Cherokee. His instruction to climb up the inside of the wing to enter the cockpit surprised me, along with the plane's small size. I had trouble fitting into the cockpit with my bulky coat. I ogled the panel full of gauges, dials, and switches. *Wow! Pilots must be brilliant to watch all of those at once!*

The engine coughed, sputtered, then ran smoothly.

"Cherokee November 21367 cleared for takeoff runway three," I heard in the headset.

The instructor added power gradually, and after a little bump, we were in the air and climbing. It was so smooth. He demonstrated the controls and some of the basics of flight. When prompted, I took the controls.

As I drove away from the airport, I reveled in the memory of each part of the flight. I loved it. All of it.

It's Not Kansas

I was in for it now—a whole new world—the military. I could take nothing of my old world with me. With nervous anticipation of great adventure in the unknown, I boarded the flight for OTS, the officer's version of basic training. During the flight, I wondered, *How will I get to the base from the airport? By taxi?*

San Antonio Airport welcomed me with heat, the scent of prairie dust, and effervescent Southern hospitality. The military host from Lackland AFB greeted us. "Ya'll wait right here, boys. Your bus will be right along." I had dropped into a different universe in Texas. I had always considered that the real world was California and New York. Discovering Texas birthed a love for the South with its slower pace, caring people, and friendliness. Increasingly, California ignored military men and women. Texas embraced them.

After several stops on the sprawling air base, the bus driver hollered, "Medina."

I shouldered my duffle bag and stepped off the bus. My eye caught the three-story beige barracks with red tile roofs, arranged in a rectangle around a grassy quad. On the fringe of the larger base, the landscape changed to rolling hills and sparse homes.

OTS? Another new, unknown world. Because the ten of us arrived in time for lunch, I lined up with the others at the chow hall. We were surrounded by skinny guys in tan uniforms, little marionettes marching around saluting each other. What a ridiculous display. I stifled my guffaw—laughing at them could hardly help my cause. They looked like the stiff soldiers at the witch's castle in *The Wizard of Oz* that chanted, "Oh-Ee-Oh!" And the cheesy black shoulder boards with the wavy line, *Give me a break!* The food, on the other hand, was great. The cherry pie made your knees weak.

My humor slowly drained away like the life of the frog in the slowly heated kettle. Little by little, my new world turned up the heat. My miserable, flea-bitten carcass was theirs. No escape.

After lunch we marched to an orientation in a dark, dilapidated theater at one end of the quad. The photo they took of me could have been used in a horror film trailer. Not only was the military environment new, I had trouble understanding what they were saying. We lined up to be processed and a clerk asked me, "Are you PCS or TDY?" I had no clue.

Brown Bar and Pilot

THE MEDINA MARINES

As a genesis of suffering, the whole complex shouted, "Welcome to the Medina Marines, idiot! Who in their right mind would sign up to be here?"

The Medina annex of Lackland AFB comprised a quad square of three-story buildings originally built in the 1950s to house those involved in the disassembly of nuclear weapons. When that operation relocated in 1965, OTS moved in. I arrived in the summer of 1966.

A fellow trainee asked, "Did you know that Air Force OTS has a reputation second only to Quantico [Marine Corps Officer Training] in toughness?"

I had no idea, but as a consequence, we called ourselves the Medina Marines.

The command building, with the commander's office (forbidden territory) and a small medical complex, stood at one end of the quad, and the chow hall and theater stood at the other end. Since the beginning of the Vietnam War, buildings had been slapped together and added rapidly.

Another trainee said, "You want to see the scene of your suffering? That big expanse of asphalt across the street is the drill pad. That is where our formations shuffle back and forth endlessly. They call it Drill and Ceremonies. See that grassy field down the street?" Much of the field remained unmowed. "You have to consistently run eight-minute-miles in the one-hundred-degree heat or they toss you out of the program on your ear." Not all could meet that pace.

Our room had a central doorway, and the door was never closed. It seemed every few minutes, like a swarm of yellow jackets, upper classmen would pop into our room to terrorize us.

Before breakfast, we labored at fatigue duty. My choice was shining brass bannisters with Brasso polish in a small can. The pungent pink-orange fluid did a great job but required elbow grease to remove all the smudges.

Also before breakfast, the upper classmen had us line up and repeatedly count off just to harass us. Each man quickly shouted the next number in line. On occasion, they would entertain themselves by having us quack off or bark off, in which we loudly imitated animal sounds.

Flight Training Officer

The first evening, our flight training officer (FTO), Lieutenant Michener, introduced himself as the person designated to shepherd us through the rigors and roadblocks of training. He was not the Air Force model in appearance. I idealized the model as lanky with blue eyes, an "aerospace" look of the wild blue yonder and an arrogant, steely gaze.

Rather, he was an academic-looking first lieutenant of medium height and build, easy to know and work with. In the artificial, chaotic world into which we had been dropped, he was sanity, reality, and a real friend. Sixteen of us met with him on our first evening to learn what was ahead.

"Gentlemen, my purpose is to get each of you through this program successfully. Tonight, I will tell you everything I know to help you do that." Patiently, he talked through all aspects of the program and what would help us succeed. He described a couple of days of issued clothing and supplies, physical training, the coming academic training, and Drill and Ceremonies, the Air Force term for close order marching. He explained that in our few off-duty hours there were rules for using the club and scant opportunities for going off the base. This cramped the style of the few men who had come with their wives. I never left the base.

He sympathized with our plight but cheered us on and prepared us for the adversities of a hostile environment. Ultimately, only one in our group failed the process due to his inability to keep up with the physical training. We noticed him falling behind but couldn't do anything to help him since he lacked the necessary stamina.

All the units of our academic training concluded with a final exam broken into a number of solos that tested individual aspects of the overall topic. You not only needed to pass the exam but also each solo. If you failed even one, it had to be retaken, which was a nuisance with the breakneck pace of training. I began my training failing a number of solos as everything was new, and I had little frame of reference. After two or three weeks, I began to get the hang of the topics and how to study, even with little time to prepare. I never failed a solo again. But my performance during the initial weeks scared my FTO.

He did not understand how determined I was. *I may bust out of this program, but it will take a few of them to carry me out. I will be kicking, screaming, scratching, and biting. Let 'em try it!*

A Plush Trap

Soon after we arrived at Medina, I filed through a cavernous warehouse that reeked of moth balls. At each stop in the line, responding to barked instructions, I picked up uniforms, shoes, and equipment, all of which would have to be displayed to perfection. Required health and grooming items came from the small exchange. The barber shop introduced me to the military haircut. In the day of the Beatles and long hair, I grieved at what was left on the floor. For an extra fee, the shop would transform my shoes to gleaming perfection. Repelled by the cost, I settled for shining my own, enduring periodic abuse from spit-shined upper classmen.

Then I launched into academic training, covering the US military, the uniform, international affairs, and a biased slant on the role of the officer. The inflated view of the officer corps left no room for the contribution of enlisted personnel. With no frame of reference for the information, I felt like a lost chicken. It was all new. The single volume, *The Air Force Officer's Guide,* saved me.

All the courses were taught in the new theater, affectionately tagged the "master bedroom." When I saw it, heaven came to mind. It was air-conditioned, and the soft chairs were tiered to the front. *Wow! This is my place.*

"Don't get comfortable, it's probably the worst atmosphere we could have for academics," Bill, a fellow trainee, alerted me.

I answered, "What are you, crazy? It's got padded seats. After running laps, the air- conditioning is amazing. What is it in here, sixty-five degrees?"

"Think about it. Your tendency to fall asleep will kill you. Watch the guys around you when their head drops or they are caught pecking corn with a head bob. From the front, the teaching staff can see everybody. The person who wakes you up will likely be staff asking for one of your demerit slips."

We had to keep three gigs (demerit slips) in an upper pocket always ready for OTS staff who noticed an infraction. Falling asleep in lecture—big infraction. Usually you could catch yourself. But, horror of horrors, if you snored or snorted, your earthly life was over.

Another danger was to be caught in an honor code violation. Common to both officer training and the US military academies, the honor code was another surprise. If caught in a lie, a man was eliminated, no questions asked. We were all competitive, straining to excel.

The temptation to compromise the truth was keen in sports, for example. *Was the volleyball out of bounds on the last volley? Did it touch the top of the net?* Beware of letting the truth slide or calling it in your favor.

UPPER CLASSMEN

"Tensh-Hut, OT [Officer Trainee]." A tan, lean upper-classman with black shoulder boards indicating an OT Captain, blocked my progress on the walk outside my barracks, not allowing me to pass. He stood close, face-to-face.

I came to terrified, ramrod attention and threw a nervous, hurried salute.

"What was that?" he barked.

"What was what, Sir?" I asked.

"That thing you did with your arm."

"A salute, Sir."

"OT Drury," his eyes zeroing in on my name tag, "in a proper salute, your hand stays on the centerline of your uniform. Do you understand that?"

"Yes, Sir."

"Watch this." He saluted with machine-like precision with the fashionable slightly cupped hand that was in vogue.

"Do you think you can do that?"

"Yes, Sir!"

"Try it, OT, and keep your hand moving on the center line of your uniform."

I did as he asked, and thus learned more about the current fashion for saluting.

"Salute again!"

"That looks better," he conceded. "And look at these gross woolies on your uniform."

Gross was the term used by the upper classmen for a massive unmilitary display perhaps endangering the entire military establishment.

He picked a small piece of lint off the front of my tan uniform shirt and flicked it away with his thumb and forefinger.

"They're disgusting. You are disgusting. And look right here, a gross cable on this button." The quarter inch of thread stood out from one of my buttonholes. "Square these things up, or you'll never make it."

"You call that a shine?" he said, looking at my shoes.

"Yes, Sir," I said, not knowing what else to say.

"You need to work harder on them or get a squared-up troop or someone at the barber shop to do it. Look at my shoes. Do you see the difference?"

I could see the deep gloss of his spit-shined shoes.

"Yes, Sir."

Finding it largely futile to waste his time on my revolting, unmilitary display, he finally looked at me with disdain and spat, "Dismissed."

Though I had been informed of the disgusting nature of my military presence, I could bask in the lasting glow of one brilliant image of military perfection.

MISSED OPPORTUNITY

My roommate Don and I were assigned to a second story room with three other officer trainees. Don was also headed toward a pilot training slot. Setting up our room became our initial challenge. Two drawers in a cabinet were intended to hold all of our earthly possessions except our uniforms, which hung overhead. Everything had to be displayed in the designated manner, spotlessly clean and pressed.

"Room, Tench-hut!" an upper classman hollered as two of them jumped into our room. What followed was a litany of how gross (remember, the acceptable word), we were.

"When are you going to get that bed squared up?"

"What's your problem? Didn't you read how those clothes are supposed to be displayed?"

"Why do you have personal items displayed in your room? Two drawers—those," he said pointing to two lower ones. "That's all you get for your disgusting personal garbage!"

"Get that stuff out of sight!"

Thoroughly revolted, they left as quickly as they came. They had long suffered the indignities of being lower classmen. Now was their chance to inflict the same on us newbies.

Our beds had to be made up so tight that a quarter would bounce off the top brown wool blanket. We had to remake them each morning, and I chose to make my bed to perfection then sleep on top of it—against house rules. I just tightened up everything in the morning.

We knew there was a pilot training eye exam the next day along with a multitude of inoculations.

"If I don't get some sleep, I'm not going to pass that eye exam tomorrow," Don said.

I dropped into bed at 2:00 a.m., exhausted, desperate for sleep. Don continued working until 4:00 a.m. We were up again at 5:00 a.m., showered and shaved in the community bathroom, then dressed and prepared for inspection by the upper classmen. Fatigue duty came next. The term seemed to designate not the measure of exertion but common labor tasks—cleaning toilets and polishing banisters. All was to be done under the harassing, inspecting gaze of upper classmen.

Back from the eye exam, Don said, "I failed my eye test. I knew if I didn't get some sleep, I would bust it."

I felt his disappointment as if it were my own. He had lost the opportunity for pilot training.

Fun in the Heat

Calisthenics in the heat drained me of life: twenty-one push-ups in thirty seconds followed by twenty sit-ups in thirty seconds. Our run of at least two miles had to be at an eight-minute-per-mile pace. Though never athletic in school—I was on the chess team—I met the requirements.

We tasted the heat on one of our first days in physical training (PT). A friend, Evans, said, "Feel that heat. I know it's over a hundred. I live near here. We shouldn't be running in this."

I answered, "It can't be. They're supposed to call off PT if it gets above one hundred."

"We got killed by the time lag," he said. "Whatever idiot monitors the temperature has to call the decision maker then that office has to call the PT officer. We've been had." We steamed in the high temps and the logjams of command.

My weight dropped from 174 to 155 during the ten weeks though I ate well. *Cherry pie? Why not a second piece?* I burned it all.

Another trial in the heat was Drill and Ceremonies, or group marching. It galled me. The thought of barking orders to others repelled me. Those who order others around should actually know what they are doing, and I didn't. My roommate Kent filled me in.

"Most of our time at drill will be in a flight, a small group of about sixteen, or a squadron, a larger group of about sixty. Learning the commands is the easy part. Leading the formation is another story, especially the squadron, or the additional rigmarole of leading a group in a parade."

I could stand leading the flight for a few minutes, but when leading the squadron, my brain screamed *I do not want to be here. Get me out of this.*

Later, in the Philippines after Vietnam, I was called aside by the squadron commander.

"Drury, there is a parade coming up for the 13th Air Force Commander. Pull out your old Drill and Ceremonies book; you are leading the squadron."

Though my answer was compliant, I burned. *This cannot be happening to me. Where are the colonels and majors? How come I get stuck with this?* I was at the bottom of the pecking order.

I immersed myself in the obscure drill regulations. Then I led 120 men around the mile-long parade ground surrounded by flame trees with brilliant orange flowers.

The 13th Air Force Commander, a major general in a small viewing stand, was the prime spectator. By some miracle, I led my unit to second place, losing to the air police, our local cops, who marched around for a living.

Maybe I retained something from OTS.

Inspection Terror

Becoming an upper classman eased some of my pain. Finally, I could walk around the Medina campus without being accosted by my snotty uppers. Life improved also when I moved into the new barracks connected with the master bedroom auditorium. Thanks to the heavenly air conditioning, I could enjoy a decent night's sleep.

Locked into my narrow OTS world, I had fallen into the habit of referring to those around me as OT Smith or OT Jones, using the last name as I would in public. Jim, a fellow classmate, suggested, "When we are with each other, let's just call each other by our first names." The growing comradery and friendship helped me relax as we endured our training journey together.

I never inflicted on the lower classmen the suffering I had endured, although it was tempting.

But, even being upper classmen could not save us from the terror of inspections. Inevitably, the dreaded time came—white glove inspection of my new barracks and our room if ours was selected. I stood sweating at attention beside my drum-tight bunk. Every inch of my uniform and room displayed military order. My shoes gleamed from layers of polish.

How bad could it be? Screamed insults? Demerits? Failure of the unmilitary interlopers to graduate? The terror loomed. All we could do was wait on the edge of the precipice.

Bam! A fist slamming into a door reverberated down the long hall. The inspectors were here. Next came a growing, ominous click, click, click in unison, as the men approached the room on the highly waxed hall floor. The taps on their shoes magnified the terror of their approach. The echo in the hall grew as they approached.

Bam! A second explosion rocked our consciousness as the fist of one of the inspectors hit our door. Three inspectors burst into the room. "Room, attention!" we shouted in unison and came to ramrod attention. In a whirlwind, the visitors examined everything, prying, looking, testing, uncovering. One examined every inch of a tan short-sleeved uniform shirt. Another bounced a quarter off my bunk. As suddenly as they had entered, they left to terrorize a few other poor saps. In our room, they struck out—they found nothing to criticize.

As we listened to the bangs and shouts from the rooms of our classmates, we could not hold back our spreading grins. We had survived until the next inspection from hell.

Hats in the Air

"**I** didn't think you were going to make it."

The comment came from Lieutenant Michener, my OTS training officer, the one who followed my progress. "You had a struggle on your hands at the beginning, didn't you?"

"Yes, I was lost," I confessed. "The new world of the military caught me flat-footed. I had no frame of reference. Failing those early solos shocked and scared me."

He did not know my determination to succeed.

On a sweltering day, September 13, 1966, the joys of graduation replaced the weeks of pain. Of the fifty-four graduates, many had advanced in rank within the program, becoming OT captains or first lieutenants. I was among the 30 percent that remained OT second lieutenants. We had survived but had not displayed skills or leadership above others. The advanced cadet rank of some soon disappeared; we'd all start in the Air Force as second lieutenants.

Using our new discipline of drill and parade, we marched in formation and presented ourselves before a small grandstand of relatives and friends. My family in California could not be present. After the ceremony, by tradition, graduates who dared threw their hats into the air. I tossed my cap within reach. I had no desire to purchase a new one.

At last, I pinned on my second lieutenant bars, and when a gleeful sergeant saluted me, he got the traditional dollar. He must have done a brisk business that day.

I called my dad from a phone booth. Emotion in his voice, he choked out, "Congratulations, Son. It is a great accomplishment. I remember the great feeling of pinning on the bars."

With a lump in my own throat I answered, "Thanks, Dad. See you in a few days."

I crammed all my things into my single green duffle bag and with my precious orders for pilot training in hand, returned to the San Francisco Bay area for a two-week leave.

In addition to my duffel bag, I had supposedly left with everything I ever needed to know about being a new Air Force officer. But another part of my baggage was an unrealistic view of my new role—the belief that an officer by virtue of his elevated rank was indeed superior to others. That view handicapped me in military teamwork based on mutual respect. There was little use for second lieutenants who did not pull their weight.

In the Cotton

"How y'all doin' today?" the lanky middle-aged gas station attendant croaked. Manning a two-pump station, he displayed the deep, weather-beaten facial creases of a farmhand. Sensing I was not a Texas boy, he drawled with genuine interest, "Where y'all from?" His charm warmed me.

The flight into Lubbock, Texas, in the fall of 1966, brought me to the home of Texas Tech University and Reese AFB. As they had in San Antonio, Texans intrigued me. Their friendliness and warmth contrasted with impersonal Californians. Recently, a friend described Texas as a tossup between hell and purgatory, but I came to consider it heaven.

On the rare occasions when I left a broken car beside the road and had to hitchhike, I found people willing to stop and help. Though normally shy and hesitant, I returned the favor by picking up hitchhikers in spite of the risk. The South exuded help and hospitality wherever needed.

Outside Lubbock, the landscape went on forever. Part of the old Llano Estacado (staked plains), it is one of the largest mesas or tablelands in North America, the elevation rising to 5,000 feet in the northwest.

Yet, the seemingly unheralded landscape is the largest cotton-growing region in the world. Its short staple cotton grows in a broad range of soils and climates. Often during harvest, tufts of cotton blew across the long, lonely road to the base.

When I entered the front gate, a WWII, B-25 bomber on a cement pedestal greeted me, designating the historic importance of Reese. The base had trained tens of thousands of pilots long before my time. A friend of mine had graduated there in the '50s.

Reporting to Reese should have exploded two of my myths about being a military officer. The first was my relationship to enlisted airmen. Having been indoctrinated into the superiority of the officer corps, I had envisioned a crowd of enlisted rabble bowing before my gleaming gold bars, crying "Unworthy! Unworthy!"

As I drove through the gate, in my eyes my second lieutenant's bars glowed. I noticed that the gate attendants were airmen. I enjoyed every millisecond of their brief, routine salute. But then I wondered why they didn't show any of the awe and wonder I was due? Their disinterest didn't stop me from wallowing in my misconceptions. *How great it is to be better than others and in the officer corps—the elite. Heck, as an officer, I'm on the top of the heap. How appropriate. I'm practically running the place. It feels wonderful to be among the truly great.*

REESE AFB

L ubbock, Texas was nicknamed the Hub City. For a large part of the South Plains, it was the economic and educational center. It was home to three universities, including the Texas Technological College (Texas Tech) Red Raiders. I was introduced to southern football traditions when I was invited to a Red Raider football game. I discovered that in contrast to the California dress code of jeans and a T-shirt, everybody came decked out in suits, dresses, and their finest. The great cheer came when the Red Raider mascot, a man dressed in a Zorro-like red costume, rode around the stadium on a black stallion.

Before World War II, Lubbock had long sought a military base nearby. Because of the worldwide conflict, Lubbock Army Airfield was created in 1942. Originally an instructor school for instrument training, it had a triangle of 6,500-foot runways. During the war, its North American T-6 advanced trainers and selection of twin-engine trainers were used to train over 7,000 pilots.

With World War II at an end, the field was placed on standby status, and the barracks became housing for veterans attending Texas Tech. On August 1, 1949, the 3500th Pilot Training Wing relocated to the field for advanced multi-engine training. The base was renamed for First Lieutenant Augustus Reese, a nearby resident, who had been killed in a bombing raid over Sardinia, Italy in 1943. The first classes, 50-A and 50-B, received advanced training in T-6 and B-25 aircraft. Runways morphed from the triangle to a full-length, north-south runway, ready for the new jet age.

During the Cold War in the 1950s, the Wing moved to providing four phases of basic flying training and added a second north-south runway. In January 1959, the wing received the T-33 bringing its training into the jet age. The stretch model of the F-80 fighter had a second seat for training. In March 1961, Reese received the T-37 Cessna twin-engine jet, nicknamed the Tweet. By the early 1960s, a third 10,500-foot runway had been added. The supersonic T-38 Talon replaced the T-33 in 1963, preparing pilots for larger and faster aircraft.

Just watching the sleek, white T-38 shoot landing patterns shot adrenalin into my veins.

Sign the Roster

My second misconception emerged in reporting for duty. I had visions of a scene from a Jimmy Stewart movie.

The worn, graying commander sits behind the desk of his fighter command, slumped in discouragement. Long has he waited for the one determined, debonair, fearless pilot who would singlehandedly win the war.

A brisk, military knock sounds at the door.

"Come in."

The dashing fighter pilot (me) boldly strides to the commander's desk. I throw a blistering salute and bark, "Lieutenant Drury reporting for duty, Sir!"

Awakening from his slumped despondency, tears glisten in the eyes of that war-hardened veteran. "At last, my son, at last you have come! Our nation is saved! The war will be won. Thank you! Thank you! We have waited so long!"

I would restrain him from kneeling and grasping my feet in gratitude.

It didn't quite happen that way. Security directed me to a nondescript, olive-drab portable building. When I entered, the World War II-era gray front office seemed empty. *Where are these people? Don't they realize the significance of this moment for their command?*

"Anybody home?" I said loudly. *Why can't I get some response? You are dealing with an officer here*, I grumped to myself. *The colonel, no doubt, has an office in the back. I'll be ushered into his office.*

An airman emerged, irritated at being interrupted. "Pilot training?" he asked. "Sign in and leave me a copy."

"Of what?" I asked, clueless.

"Sign this roster and place a copy of your orders underneath the stack already there," he explained, patronizing my ignorance before again disappearing. I signed and shuffled through my papers for a copy of orders that assigned me to undergraduate pilot training.

Only one of us in the quiet office was gainfully employed, and it wasn't me.

On reporting, though my orders said my pilot training class would not start until December, I hoped I would be snapped up by an early class—one with an instructor desperate for a young, hot pilot. Instead, I learned I was "casual" along with a host of others, hanging around on a leash, a useless nuisance to everyone. I was waiting, just waiting for a pilot training class.

I still had to report in twice daily in case some ridiculous errand could be concocted by some unit or somebody on base had a use for the useless.

SEttLinG In

My new home, base housing, was a two-story World War II-era barracks, painted olive drab, on the edge of the base. Though dated, it soon felt like home for my fourteen months in training. I shared the space with Don, a husky, muscular trainee and a Lubbock native. His parents worked one of the many cotton farms in the area. Our quarters contained a small living room, two small bedrooms, and a small kitchen. Perfect!

Whether flying or academics were first in the day, we started early. When scheduled to fly, I have always battled a nervous anticipation of responsibility and having to perform. Since the Officers Club was at the other end of the base, I usually picked up something to eat on the run in the mornings. So began my love affair with a donut or pastry and coffee for breakfast, usually purchased in one of the long buildings that housed T-37 and T-38 training.

Once training started, the pace was so intense that normally I fought the tendency to crash in the evenings. The academic material covered all aspects of flying: weather, the principles of flight, and safe operation of the aircraft. It was all new but all fascinating.

One evening Don said, "I'm headed home for dinner at the house. Why don't you come with me?"

We drove through miles of cotton fields to a spacious white frame house surrounded by loads of farm equipment. Inside I discovered a warm-hearted family with doors and hearts as big as Texas. They welcomed me as one of their own.

Don's dad led the way, "Jon, great to have you here. I hear you're a California boy. What do you think of Texas so far?"

I gave him the good news.

During the amazing meal of fried chicken and mashed potatoes, I asked, "Can someone pass the bread?" They all looked at me puzzled and asked, "Cornbread or light bread?" I had never known there were two kinds of bread until they convinced me. I came to love the texture, aroma, and flavor of Southern cornbread.

For transportation, I picked up a humble, dependable little Plymouth Valiant that performed well. Later, though, a bigger, more comfortable car close to my automotive idea—a Pontiac Catalina—caught my eye. Mechanically, it proved a disaster. A broken fuel pump had to be replaced with an electrical fuel pump which served as a constant buzzing reminder of my impulsive car purchase.

Little by little, I settled into my new home and the rapid drumbeat pace of training.

Hanging Around

Everywhere I went on base there were pilot trainees in full-length gray flight suits, their caps at a jaunty angle. They talked excitedly, making flying and formation motions with their hands. They were pilots. I was nobody; just a "casual." Everyone knew a casual officer, waiting for pilot training, was as odious as a leprous pariah and useless to everybody. Finally, I gained work at the computer office.

I faced a mountain of computer cards, each card eighty columns wide, full of punched holes. The cards fed a computer that tracked student pilots, recorded what flights they had completed, then generated options for the next flight. It might spit out two visual flight rules (VFR) rides, a solo flight, and an instrument flight.

The student's instructor chose the flight best for that day. In bad weather he might pick an instrument flight. If tied up with another student, he might assign a solo. The computer office manned by enlisted, noncommissioned officers (NCOs) and officers hummed with efficiency. Their effectiveness impressed me.

Next, I was asked to work for the Flight Safety Office nearer the heartbeat of the base—flight operations. Engines were periodically flaming out (losing all power) on the T-37 Tweet after two specific maneuvers: spin preventions and spin recoveries. An aircraft spin, or tailspin, is the rapid descent of an airplane in a steep spiral after loss of lift to the wings. A spin can prove deadly. If control cannot be restored, then both pilots have to bail out. If there are glitches in the bailout, ejection could be fatal.

Handling spins was essential for a pilot. Spin recovery training used spins, intentionally induced, to teach proper recovery techniques. In the T-37, the technique had resulted from a rash of spin-related accidents and several fatalities. Stopping a spin and pulling out of it was often a violent, jarring maneuver. The pilot applied rudder opposite the direction of the spin for one turn then banged the control stick forward and held it there to break the spin. The technique might produce a smooth recovery, but it also might produce zero or negative G forces or flip the aircraft inverted. At times, the recovery brought the dust, dirt, screws, etc. up from the floor of the aircraft into the pilot's face. The violence of the maneuver had at times induced compressor stalls or flameouts.

I tracked back through stacks of incidents throughout Air Training Command (ATC) when engines had flamed out due to the maneuvers and tabulated the results. I enjoyed the project then turned over what I learned to the directors of Flight Safety. They, in turn, taught safer operation to flight instructors throughout the system.

I shuddered to think of someone losing his life in a training accident.

Party Hearty?

"Let's go down to the Stag Bar."

The invitation of my friend recommended a location that fostered the fighter pilot mindset and swagger. A small, smoky bar, it connected to the back of the Officers' Club. Socializing, rolling dice for drinks, and bragging of conquests relieved the pressure of training for some. Though I admired the camaraderie of friends, it felt claustrophobic; it was not my place. I had always been a loner, insecure about my place with others. Because of hurts in childhood, I came into adulthood reasoning, *You never know who will stick you.* I was wary of close relationships. Time at the bar also seemed a waste when I was scrambling to keep pace with the demands of training.

Even those who socialized there or elsewhere learned to live by the rule: eight hours from bottle to throttle. It meant eight hours alcohol-free before piloting an aircraft. The gentleman's rule applied to all Air Force flying, including training.

The partying tendencies of our group emerged at a class meeting. "What should we do for our next class party?"

One of our single guys said, "Let's get some strippers in here."

At first it seemed the idea would win the day though it showed immaturity and poor judgment. Since I was not among the more visible class members, I hesitated to speak up. John Crotty, one of my friends, sounded the voice of reason.

"Many of us have wives and families. I don't think it's a good idea." He was one of the influential guys in the class, and they listened to reason. John and class president Chet Thatcher always represented the best in values and character. Both served tours flying F-105 Thuds out of Thailand while I was flying C-7A Caribous in Vietnam.

The Officers' Club hosted the occasions of our formal dining-in. Dressed in our formal mess dress, the equivalent of a tuxedo, the occasion featured contests and games. On one occasion, a friend from the Alabama National Guard broke his arm in an arm-wrestling contest. When the commander of his home unit heard about it, his angry expressions to our commander were colorful: "What in hell are you people doing down there injuring my boy?" It meant delayed graduation for this pilot.

Some of our guys tried the Cotton Club on the west side of town. It was known not only as a watering hole but also a place that had hosted and stoked the careers of many rock n' roll and country music greats. Though I never got there, I began to love the country music sound.

BEVERLY

Through Vern Sivage, a good friend at Texas Tech, I visited a small Baptist church in Lubbock. My previous contact with Baptist churches had been scant. In college, five of us with little talent sang together as the Five Lemons for a group of Baptists. We were not invited back.

The church had a college and career group that included college students from Tech as well as young career men and women. I particularly enjoyed the upbeat, informative studies, hilarious songs, fun activities, and members with big personalities. On some evenings, the church cooked a big dinner and served fifty or sixty in the group.

At one of their home socials, I met Beverly, a Texas Tech freshman. She was a cutie—a pretty, modest, quiet eighteen-year-old with big brown eyes.

I was eating a sandwich in a doorway when she was asked by a girlfriend, "Do you want to meet Jon? He's a pilot out at Reese."

She answered, "Of course."

My friend turned to me and said, "Jon, this is Beverly, an English major at Tech."

"Whoops! I flunked English in high school," I replied.

With her shy smile and deep brown eyes, she answered my question about her home. A freshman at Tech, she had just graduated second in her class from a large high school in Odessa, Texas.

After the visit, I reflected, *Wow! I'm interested.* I began calling her, though neither one of us can remember how I got her number.

During the Christmas holidays, I invited her to a group party—a dinner out—and we began dating. I invited Beverly to receptions at the base and since she was very mature for her eighteen years, she fit right in.

My friend John, who had wisely nixed the strippers, said, "If you weren't dating her, I would ask her out."

She was popular at school, too. If I wanted a date, I had to ask at least two weeks ahead. Sometimes I heard, "I'm sorry, I already have a date for that night." Some sleaze ball had edged me out.

Our favorite date was cruising the loop—driving the loop highway around Lubbock, going nowhere. Talk about a cheap date. While cruising, we'd sing the crazy songs of our group: "Silver Threads and Golden Needles," sung with appropriate southern accent and "Chug a Lug, Chug a Lug." We had a fabulous time going in circles.

Our deepening friendship made it the most satisfying dating relationship I had known. But outings and phone calls burned up Beverly's valuable study time, a sacrifice for a solid-A student.

Could we have a future together?

FLIGHt SUIt

Preparing for my pilot training class, I again filed through a warehouse reeking of mothballs and picked up flight suit, boots, flying gloves, and equipment. I reveled in my own coveted gray flight suit, size 42-L. It felt like heaven. I examined every inch of it—every inspector's tag in the pockets. I tried all the zippers. *Wow! Look at all the pockets.* I now had an identity and a place.

Flight suit, boots, and flying gloves felt cool and comprised our flying uniform for the first phase of training. In the next phase, we would add a helmet, oxygen mask, and parachute pack, which would be neither comfortable nor good-looking. Still later, for the T-38 Talon, I would add a tight G suit from my waist down. It inflated with air and squeezed the lower body to keep consciousness and vision under higher g-forces. But for my beginning in the T-41, this gear was not necessary. I would settle for just a flight suit.

I wore a student squadron patch on my right breast and a white name patch on my left breast. Later I wore a squadron patch on my left shoulder. Required dog tags hung around my collar, tucked inside the flight suit. I often wore a colorful silk scarf around my neck, a throwback to World Wars I and II where a fighter pilot's head was on a swivel, constantly looking for the "Hun in the sun." The scarf protected your neck from chafing and rubbing against your collar. Besides, it looked so cool. Air Force blue became my color of choice.

While in the cockpit, I loved the convenience of the scads of pockets in my flight suit. I stocked them with everything I needed in flight: pen, radio frequency books, and departure and approach instructions. Often, something I stuck in my flight suit made my job easier. One of those items became a rechargeable, compact flashlight, which helped me locate items in a dark cockpit at night when interior lighting had to be limited to preserve vision.

In Vietnam, the comfortable gray flight suit was banned, and we had to wear the itchy, hot, Nomex suit instead. Though miserable in the heat, it was fire resistant and saved lives and limbs during crashes and fires.

Even when I had to wear it all day, my new flight suit afforded amazing comfort. It was home.

Class 68-D

My smile broadened as I read the note. I had a pilot training class. Though it had seemed forever, I had waited only five weeks.

Having survived the grinding anonymity of being a casual, Class 68-D formed, the fourth class to graduate in 1968. We numbered seventy-four men. Pilot training would take place in three phases, the first being the T-41 Mescalero, a military version of the dependable, single-engine Cessna 172.

In the second phase, the Cessna T-37, "Tweety Bird," "Dogwhistle" or "Tweet" was a twin-engine jet with side-by-side seating for the instructor and student. It received its monikers from the whistling sound the engines made when the throttles were retarded in the traffic pattern for landing. Modified for combat, the A-37 Dragonfly would serve in Vietnam. I could not foresee that there I would lose one of my friends, Dave, flying this modified version on a combat mission.

In the final phase of training, we went supersonic with the Northrop T-38 Talon, a rocket with wings. Even taxiing, the sleek white plane charged you with energy.

My training days were split. My class was divided into two sections, and I alternated between flying mornings with afternoon academic classes and the opposite schedule the following week. Either way, the pace was nonstop as I gained knowledge and experience, all of it new.

Each step of my training was led by Chet, my class leader, already a captain because of prior service. Wise, measured, and insightful, he respected everyone and represented the finest in values and character. He was someone I trusted and could follow without hesitation.

In addition to academics and flying, we had athletics—never my strong suit. I hobbled around for days after spraining my ankle in volleyball, typical of my clumsiness.

Everything was new and fascinating, but since I had no parallel experience to fall back on, I faced the constant terror of missing or forgetting critical information. Classes taught weather, principles of flight, aircraft mechanics, and aircraft performance. Jumping out of the books, we encountered reality on the flight line where we started from scratch learning the T-41.

An uncomfortable hurdle appeared on my first flight in the small cockpit. My instructor sat next to me on the right, directing, instructing, and criticizing. When he climbed in, his jacket touching mine, I wanted to scream. His presence at close quarters violated my needed space.

I purchased a pilot log book from the Bell Flying Service. The record shows my first flight was December 12, 1966, and lasted one hour. I kept this treasure.

THE AIR FORCE WAY

N ew to the flying game and curious, I asked Chet, my flight commander, about our first aircraft.

"What we fly is the T-41A Mescalero," he answered. "They started using them in 1965. It's a dependable sweetheart, maybe the best trainer around. It's the military version of the Cessna 172 Skyhawk you see everywhere. The only change is a more efficient climb propeller and an Air Force paint job. Cessna is building a ton of them."

This initial phase had twin purposes. One we knew; the other we did not know. The first purpose was introduction to the Air Force way of flying.

Our senior military instructors tweaked us with this: "It is better to arrive with no flying experience so there is nothing to unlearn. The Air Force way of flying is superior to any alternative."

What was that particular way of flying? Based on the disciplines that were reinforced, my guess from repeated instruction was:

- Exactness as opposed to approximate being acceptable.
- Checklists to be sure that every important item is covered.
- Thorough knowledge of the aircraft and what it will do.

- Meticulous performance of all procedures.
- Diligent preparedness for emergencies learned by rote.
- Courage, aggressiveness, and teamwork.
- Absolute commitment to the mission, to the death.

The majority of us would be initiated into this Air Force way of flying.

The second purpose of this phase of training was kept from us. It was the screening of all the candidates. The instructors had to eliminate those who were the slowest to adjust to the aggressive military flight and training atmosphere. Training moved rapidly, and there was little sympathy for those who were slow to learn or did not have the physical and mental abilities to learn and perform quickly. They needed to prepare those who perform for demanding operational flying assignments. Each man had to be trained to fly anything in the Air Force inventory.

As one who had no flying experience, I felt the breakneck pace of training. I studied as diligently as I could and performed the flying tasks the best I could, based on what my instructor said. Fortunately, it was enough.

Later, this first phase for all pilot training was consolidated at Hondo, Texas. After successful completion of this first phase, the trainee went to one of the pilot training bases for the rest of his training.

BELL FLYING SERVICE

I itched for training to begin—the dream seemed possible, yet the challenge scared the life out of me.

Because two phases of jet training jammed the flight line at Reese, our first phase of training in the Cessna T-41 began not on base, but at a nearby airport. The civilian training site we used was at Lubbock Municipal Airport perhaps ten miles from Reese.

Contracted by the Air Force, Bell Flying Service provided training buildings, offices, a hangar, civilian instructors, and ramp space. My crowded training room held ten heavy, gray tables arranged down a rectangular room around a central aisle.

When my section flew in the morning, I boarded the bus at 6:30 a.m., often in the dark, decked out in my pilot garb. I vibrated with the nervous energy of anticipation. All of us were arrogant, pretentious, in our own eyes already steely-eyed fighter pilots blasting the hapless enemy out of the sky.

What will the day hold? Will I measure up? Will I remember what I need for my flight? Will I be able to perform the maneuvers?

Curtis Crump, a hard-drinking country boy, revised my image of a straight-laced flight instructor. About fifty years old, of average height, and with salt-and-pepper hair and a heavy southern drawl, he was a veteran flight instructor. His ruddy weather-beaten face proclaimed years of flying as well as his love of Jack Daniels. Eight trainees gathered around Crump's government-issued table. Though jammed with students, his casual, unflappable good humor said he had been doing this for decades—born in the saddle.

My military flight instructors steeled themselves to teach me the Air Force way to fly. It made no difference that I was only flying a glorified Cessna 172, a sturdy four-place trainer now tweaked for the military and painted silver and black.

I temporarily accepted the dictum of my Air Force supervisors that it was better to arrive having done no flying at all rather than enduring the curse of not flying the Air Force way. But their flawed premise surfaced when each man with flying experience invariably did far better than we novices did. John Crotty, who already had his commercial pilot certificate, became one of the top members of the class. His class standing rewarded him with a coveted assignment: flying the F-105 Thunderchief, "Thud," out of Korat Air Base in Thailand.

WHY IN THE WORLD?

The flat patchwork quilt of green farms, brown open land, and oil pumper units stretched forever around Lubbock. In West Texas, called the "oil patch," thousands of oil-pumping units moved rhythmically up and down like giant bugs feeding. In the blue above this scene, our flying instruction took place.

In the air, my class used the call sign "Bell," Curtis Crump's call sign being "Bell-Five-O." Students had numbers corresponding to their instructor; mine was "Bell-Five-Two." When we called to tell the airport we were inbound, we did so from above a tavern out in the country, called Pinkies. My solo entry call was, "Lubbock tower, Bell Five Two Pinkies, inbound." The call pinpointed my location for the tower and my intentions: a forty-five-degree entry to downwind, the outside leg of the landing pattern rectangle. Tower then assigned a different runway if they wished but always kept us separated from the main north-south runway used by commercial airliners.

Crump patiently worked through the training syllabus, including not only skills necessary for any pilot, but the mindset necessary to survive in the flying and military universe. I wondered how he could teach the same principles hundreds or thousands of times, yet maintain his good humor.

I was handicapped by never having seen the maneuvers nor understanding the reason for them. Often in some strange maneuver I puzzled, *Why in the world does he want me to do that?* He might as well have said, "Jump up and down, rub your stomach, and chant, 'the moon is made of green cheese'!" I practiced maneuvers in which elevation, heading, airspeed, and power settings were varied at the same time. I later realized that he was teaching essential aircraft control.

He also assigned practice traffic patterns over sections of road, imaginary runways, adjusting for the effect of wind on the path of the aircraft. I learned to "crab," flying at an angle into the wind to keep a consistent track over the landscape.

Crosswind landings set my nerves on edge—trying to land smoothly on an east-west runway with a significant north-south wind. Crump taught a wing-low landing technique, lowering one wing into the wind during the landing approach to touchdown.

Pilots not flying remained at the tables, studied their course materials, checklists, or academic subjects.

My calves ached from working the rudder pedals. I could barely use them, yet use them I had to as training pushed forward. I lived in misery, but complaining was useless. I suffered in silence and told nobody.

MOnKEYS Can FLY

My instructor turned to me in flight: "Did you see anything as we came into the traffic pattern?"

"No," I replied.

"You completely missed another Bell aircraft trying to enter." I heard the frustration in his voice.

I was so busy with the details of flying inside my own cockpit, I'd missed the Cessna right next to me. Hadn't even seen it! It showed me the importance of continually scanning for other aircraft. I failed the ride because of the lapse. I then took a check flight. It was called an "elim ride"—if you failed it, you were eliminated from pilot training. But I passed and was allowed to continue in the program.

One day I came to my table and noticed two of the students were missing. I didn't think much of it for a couple of days. Then I quietly asked about the missing students. They had busted out of the program. It was consistent with the Air Force way of doing things. Unless you "hacked the program," you were out. Between our two sections, seventy-four men entered the T-41 phase but only fifty-four completed it. More than a quarter of the men who entered that phase had been eliminated.[2]

Though it was the military way, those who failed to qualify were devastated. What seemed certain glory and fulfillment was snuffed out in a brief elimination check ride. They might have the possibility of navigator training, but that prospect brought little comfort in the loss of the greater goal of being an Air Force pilot. A tall country boy shared his agony with me over the death of his dreams when he was eliminated. I suffered my own pain when I was tossed out in the T-38 phase, but then rejoiced when I was returned to training.

According to the Air Force, student pilots were a dime a dozen, so officers didn't waste any time babying a weak trainee. There was very little recourse for a student who needed extra work on some phase. The program continued—relentlessly. Invariably, all who had entered the program with flying experience or their private or commercial pilot's license graduated and moved on to the next phase. They had the head start the rest of us needed.

To keep us humble, we often heard the phrase "You can teach a monkey to fly!" Monkeys had the jump on us in intelligence and skill.

Raining Mudballs

"What do you see yonder down to the south?" Curtis Crump, my flight instructor, asked in my headset.

My eyes widened. "It looks like rolling brown clouds—a big brown wall," I answered.

"Welcome to a West Texas dust storm, Son. Better put us on the ground. It's moving a bit faster than weather said it would."

In the home of the yellow rose, violent weather often impacted our flying. We'd spot a wall of dust ten or fifteen miles distant and smell it in the air. If it was moving toward us, we had limited time to land.

Once the storm hit, another surprise greeted me back at my barracks. I ran my finger over the brown arm of an armchair. Pure grit. Despite locked doors and windows, the dust had seeped through every window and door crack, dusting furniture, dishes, and counters. Nothing I could do would keep out the fine dust.

When I drove in a dust and rain storm, mudballs pelted my windshield.

The black wall of thunderstorms posed a greater danger than dust, and they often moved fast. In one dangerous black storm in Midlothian,

Texas, I wrestled the bird against rising winds, landed, then moved the aircraft into the hangar. On the ramp, even if you tied the aircraft down with heavy chains, a blown tumbleweed could cause scratches or damage. With light aircraft in Texas, nobody played with thunderstorms.

A microburst, a localized downdraft in a thunderstorm, can topple grown trees.

Then there are hailstorms—golfball-, baseball-, or even softball-sized hail. We arrived back at Beverly's home at one point to the eerie sight of all the trees stripped of their leaves by hail.

Wrestling with a light airplane in turbulence and strong winds challenged me, but time and again I returned to Crump's wing-low landings. The technique allowed us to land safely by touching down first on the low main gear.

One early morning in training, darkened clouds and rain threated. Would we be able to fly? A flight instructor launched in a T-37 to see firsthand. His eyes on the clouds, a flash of white spelled disaster. It was too late to turn, and at 200 miles an hour, a large sandhill crane hit and exploded his plexiglass bubble canopy. Though seriously injured by the crane and pieces of canopy, he landed successfully. Tragically, he died of his injuries.

On the ramp, the airplane with its shattered canopy and bloody cockpit stunned us. I agonized, *How could someone die? This is training. We're not even in combat yet.*

Texas and flying were a unique mix with their own dangers.

It's All Yours, Champ

"**I**t's all yours, champ. Take it around three times."

That morning my instructor and I climbed into T-41 tail number N5122F, a number I will never forget, and worked on my landings. After one landing, Crump said "Take'er to the ramp, Son."

Stopped on the ramp, Crump opened his door and got out.

What in the world is he doing? I thought, shocked. Then he told me to take it around three times, solo. Any reasoning mortal would have raised issues. *Do I really know enough to fly this thing by myself? Do I really know what I'm doing?*

In reality, I was not sure why everything worked the way it did, but I had apparently gained skills enough to take off and land. After all, you can teach a monkey to fly.

Changing to a solo call sign, Tower cleared me for takeoff. When I broke ground on my takeoff, exhilaration took over. Though invisible to the earthbound, I was overwhelmed by freedom, joy, and a sense of accomplishment. Conservative and restrained by nature, I couldn't help the grin that broke out on my face. I wanted to shout. I wanted to sing.

I owned the sky. I owned the earth, which was appropriately below me, bowing in obeisance to me, the intrepid aviator.

Flying solo after ten hours and fifty minutes of instruction compared favorably with what the other students had done. I doubt that many soloed with fewer than ten hours. In the landings, I repeated what I had learned and returned to the hangar victorious. Nobody said, "Wipe that stupid grin off your face."

Nothing would ever be the same. The sky was bluer, the grass greener, and I was convinced I was one of the most skillful "sticks" aviation had ever produced. At last I was master of the skies—a full-fledged aviator.

On occasion, in some parts of training, reality did hit: *I don't know what in the world I am doing.* I should have asked more questions, but I was hindered by embarrassment. When mystified, I followed what I had learned by rote and gradually got the picture. Years later, flying operational aircraft, all of the procedures sank in and came naturally.

After a total of thirty hours of flying, I graduated from the T-41 phase. Students, instructors, and supervisors met for a final celebration. Some students thanked their instructors with gifts. Crump got some Jack Daniels.

For me, N5122F was a bird I would never forget. I carefully inscribed the number in my treasured black flight log.

THE TWEEt

With a tarnished aluminum exterior and thrashed interior, my first jet, the Cessna T-37, had been a training mainstay for a long time. Years of instruction had worn, scratched, and tarnished the interior. As in the T-41, student and instructor sat side by side, the student on the left and instructor on the right.

Called the Tweet, also the Tweety Bird, or Dogwhistle, the T-37 received its moniker because of the whistling sound it made in the overhead landing pattern when the throttle was retarded in the pitchout, the steep forty-five-degree banking turn made to the downwind leg of the traffic pattern after entry on "initial."

For the T-37, I wore a solid flight helmet with a sunglass visor that could be lowered to reduce glare. I could choose an emblem to decorate my helmet and chose a design used by my flying buddies from the Alabama National Guard. Combined with an oxygen mask, which covered my nose and mouth, a parachute, and flying gloves, an oven of Texas heat enveloped me on the flight line. I perspired buckets. None of the equipment was optional no matter how miserable I felt. I did not yet wear a G suit. That wouldn't come until the T-38. For initial cranking up on the ramp and taxiing, we nearly suffocated.

Once I was strapped in, a growing whine told me I had a good start on the engines. Before I taxied, the crew chief would hold up two pins with red tags for the landing gear, showing they had been removed. The pins prevented accidental gear collapse on the ground. We gently pulled the safety pins out of our ejection seats, held our breath, and held them up for the crew chief to see. Now the seats were hot, ready for ejection at altitude. If the seats malfunctioned and fired on the ground, we would die. The T-37 did not have a zero-zero (zero speed, zero altitude) ejection seat, one that even while the plane was sitting on the ramp would rocket the pilot up high enough for a successful ejection.

At last, taxiing relieved some of my suffering. We could taxi fast and with the clamshell canopy open, scoop some air into the cockpit. This provided some heavenly relief from my agony. More complete cooling arrived once the canopy was closed and the engines accelerated for takeoff. Finally, heavenly air conditioning flowed.

Aleksander Solzhenitsyn once observed that a man who is warm cannot possibly understand one who is cold. Perhaps one who is air-conditioned fails to appreciate one who is sweltering.

Nothing but Jets

An endless row of sleek, supersonic Northrop T-38s and silver Cessna T-37s filled the mile-long flight line at Reese. Not a prop plane in the bunch. Just seeing that many jets ramped my adrenalin.

Graduation from T-41s released me from propeller purgatory to the flight line at Reese for the T-37, my next phase of training. All the ground instruction for that bird happened in one long building while T-38 training happened in another. No more bus trips to Lubbock Muni; I had come to the big time—flying jets.

My class, 68-D, was still divided into two sections, twenty-seven students each. I did not know many in the other section. We were seldom in the same place at the same time. Other rooms in the building held additional classes and sections, each at a different point in training.

As at Lubbock Muni, each instructor had a heavy gray table with room for his four or five students. But now our instructors were veteran Air Force pilots instead of civilians, some back from combat and most former fighter pilots. I viewed them with awe. They were my heroes.

In my training room, a rack against the wall held computer-generated flying missions for each student. I had learned the system when I worked in the computer office. Each card specified an instructional ride or a solo if the student had soloed. The solo rides were used to practice the maneuvers we learned.

My T-37 instructor, Kent TeKrony, was a cool fighter-pilot type. Of medium height with dark hair, he was quiet but so confident he always seemed to have the same stone face. A veteran instructor, he was a fighter pilot by instinct and unflappable. His unswerving confidence seemed to say, "In flying, I've seen it all and done it all. Want to try me?"

In contrast, a few instructors lived in fear that a trainee was trying to kill them. I flew with an older major. To keep me from doing anything risky, he came close to "caging the stick": circling it with his hands to protect himself from something stupid I might do. But he lived to fly another day.

Kent sometimes got frustrated with imbeciles, including yours truly. When that occurred, he simply shouted, "Put your hands in your lap!" I quickly released the stick, my face reddening in humiliation. The limit of the instructor pilot's endurance had been reached.

He then flew a while and regained his shattered composure. I grieved that I had failed to learn the technique being taught.

When his patience and composure were sufficiently restored, he again gave me—the student imbecile—control of the plane.

JOYS OF THE DOGWHISTLE

My heart raced. *Why waste the opportunity? Could I?*

The fleecy white cloud beckoned me in my first solo in the twin-jet T-37. Slicing under the cloud, I hauled back the stick to loop all the way around the cloud.

Yeehaw! Luckily my satisfied grin and my dance with the cloud could not be transmitted back to my base. It was forbidden to fly within 500 feet of the fluffy stuff. Other planes on instruments, including airliners, flew through the white mist. They hoped to avoid anything solid. I was kind of hazy on the rules anyway.

Back on the ground, I got dunked. Guys in my flight celebrated my solo by submerging me and my perspiration-soaked flight suit in a humble cattle tank. But the glow of satisfaction could not be washed out.

Though solo missions freed me from prying eyes, it also robbed me of help in a pinch. Later, when practicing landing patterns solo in a practice area, I repeatedly got a left main gear red light. *Is my left gear there? Has it fallen off? Is it jammed and dangerous for landing?*

I radioed operations with my dilemma.

They answered, "Moxnix One-Two, return to Reese. A chase plane is going to look over your gear."

An instructor pilot (IP) flew repeatedly around my bird, while I lowered and raised the gear.

"Moxnix, despite the red light, I can't see anything wrong. Make a normal landing. Emergency and fire will be in place if anything goes south."

Anything could have happened on landing, but it didn't. Later in the day, a sergeant in coveralls found me.

"Lieutenant Drury, we found the problem. It was just a broken wire."

Then came a lesson about flying and human physiology. In another solo, exhausted from the pace of training, I pulled too many Gs. I grayed-out, or lost all my vision. It was like a dark curtain fell top to bottom over my sight. I could see nothing.

Dear God, how am I going to fly this thing blind?

I could not recall ever hearing about the phenomena of graying out. I could feel the stick, and all my other senses were in place. Excessive g-forces can cause loss of vision due to low blood pressure in the brain.

Because the airplane was, more or less, trimmed up and in balance, with reduced power, the aircraft entered a falling-leaf mode without stick or rudder movements.

It seemed like it took forever to gradually regain my sight, slowly, but may have been a minute or two, or less. I never forgot the stark terror, but I had learned something about flying, exhaustion, pulling Gs, and physiology.

Embarrassed, I told nobody.

Loss of My Cheerleader

"Lieutenant Drury, call the chaplain's office."

The note came from a clerk in our training building. I asked my instructor, "Can I go check on this?"

With a compassionate tone the chaplain's office said, "I am sorry, Lieutenant. Your father has died."

I reflected, *At least he doesn't have to suffer any more.* I remembered my dad dancing in the living room with small children in his arms. Another joyful memory was his coming home from work with Bireley's orange drink for the kids. I remembered car trips with dad when just the two of us got to talk about life.

Now my greatest cheerleader was gone.

He died in a mental hospital where his health had continued to deteriorate. His road downhill was complicated by diabetes and vascular disease—poor circulation. He had been a three-pack-a-day smoker from his teens. Amputation of a leg landed him in a wheelchair, a difficulty because our house had two flights of stairs.

Then there was the decline of his mental health. Though highly intelligent—he had received his master's degree from San Francisco

State—his irrational behavior and demands grew. The longer story is that dad's mother had died giving birth to him and his disabled twin. His father died when he was five, and his twin brother died when he was twelve. All contributed to my dad's smoking and poor habits as a teen.

He entered Agnews State Hospital under veteran's benefits. While I was in the first phase of Undergraduate Pilot Training (UPT), his second leg was amputated.

Between OTS and pilot training, I had visited Dad. I found a caring staff and dad in his wheelchair, highly interested in my upcoming pilot training.

He carried his favorite large folio book on the Air Force with him everywhere in his chair. Knowing his fascination with aviation, I had given him the book inscribed, "To Dad, Love, Jon."

To anyone who would listen he said, "My son, Jon, is in Texas training to be an Air Force pilot. He gave me this book."

When I told my pilot training commander about the death, he said, "You are due for a T-37 cross country with an IP. Why don't you and he fly back there for the service?"

We flew through Luke AFB west of Phoenix then to Hamilton Field in the San Francisco Bay area. I attended the service and comforted my mother and family. In my dress blues, I shared my favorite memories of Dad.

One of my treasures is the Air Force book with the plain shopping bag cover that dad kept in his chair. It is a memento of my greatest cheerleader.

ALL OVER †HE SKY

"You've got it, Stick," Kent, my IP said in an introductory formation flight.

I had watched him and another instructor demonstrate perfection as our two gleaming silver planes moved as one in the sunlight, turning, climbing, rolling. The perfection of it stunned me. Both birds remained tucked together tightly in the same position.

Now it was my turn to try. *What could be hard about this? The airplane almost flies itself. This should be easy.*

When I took the black control stick, the rock-solid formation disintegrated. I ballooned above my position, then overcorrected and dumped below it. Every control I entered was too much. Then I was all over the sky, on the edge of collision and disaster.

"I've got it," my instructor said, rescuing us. "Not quite as easy as it looks, is it?" Kent quipped, a knowing smile creasing his stone face.

"How did I screw up?" I asked, wiping the sweat off my forehead with my flying glove.

"Watch how small my control movements are," he said.

That was something I had missed. Amazingly, the stick was always moving with small changes, not the large ones I had used.

Viewed at airshows from the grandstands looking up, formation flying looks insanely easy. It took me weeks of formation training to adjust to the constant small changes necessary to fly smoothly as a wingman. Though my first attempt was poor, this I loved.

"What do you think are the challenges of being the lead ship?" Kent asked in a follow-up lesson. I had no idea.

"You need to lead smoothly," he continued, "so your wing men can follow you."

Puzzled about one aspect of formation, I asked, "What if the leader makes a mistake? Shouldn't you watch out for yourself?"

"There should be two smoking holes in the ground," he answered, "or four if you are in a four-ship formation."

"You can't be serious," I replied.

Originally, his answer startled me and made no sense. Further in training, I finally accepted the truth of the shocking statement. The wing aircraft always follows the lead no matter what. It was all tied to completing the mission as a unit, as a formation, not as an individual aircraft.

A fighter pilot I talked to had flown a strafing mission into Tay Ninh in Vietnam. When back on the ground, his leader commented, "Wasn't that ground fire intense?"

The wingman answered, "I didn't even see it!" His eyes were only on the lead ship.

Good wingman.

POINT THE NOSE UP

"Let 'er go, Bud."

My instructor's words came as my sleek white T-38 Talon rumbled in place, aimed straight down the 10,000-foot runway. It wanted to run. At military power, 100 percent, it was all the power the plane had except for the afterburner. That was next. The burner dumped raw fuel into the engine in massive quantities.

Graduating from the T-37 brought us further into the big time, the T-38: my final phase of training and the most demanding. At the speed of the T-38, just to turn 180 degrees in the air took two miles. Things happened fast.

Built like a fighter, its swept-back wings and tons of power made the T-38 a flying hot rod. All the gauges centered on a heads-up display—many flight indicators located together—to minimize glances inside the cockpit. The two cockpits were tandem, front and back: I in the front, my instructor in back.

Rocking at military power for my first takeoff, I checked the gauges to be sure I had no fire light or out-of-limits indications. At my IP's word, I moved the throttles forward over the friction detent. With a boom, the afterburner, a tunnel of flame, rocketed me down the runway. In a few seconds, my airspeed indicator passed 105 knots, 120 miles per hour, and I rotated the nose up.

My heart pounded.

I lifted off the runway, pointed the nose up and pegged the vertical velocity indicator. At one time, the Talon held the world time-to-climb record.

I was breathless after my rocket ride almost straight up to seven miles above the earth. Then came the next surprise.

"Wanna try supersonic?" my instructor asked.[27]

"You've got to be kidding," I answered.

I advanced the power and following a slight bump, my instructor asked, "What does your mach meter say?"

"One point two, Sir,"

"Where was the sonic boom?"

"I don't know."

"We don't hear it, but everyone else does," he explained.

Back in my classroom, I dutifully filled out the supersonic log, the record of my breaking the sound barrier. The Air Force could then reimburse residents with shattered windows or terrified hens that refused to lay.

In Muleshoe, Texas, Farmer Jones shook his fist at the heavens outside his broken plate glass window. "Dang flyboys."

I Bust Out

"I'm sorry, Son. You failed your elimination ride. You are no longer in pilot training, but keep your flight gear until the board makes a final decision."

Both of us were exhausted from the flight. I sat with the chunky, graying flight examiner. Elimination from pilot training hit like a sledgehammer. *It can't be. How could it have happened this quickly? Where do I go now?*

My check pilot tried to comfort me. "I'm sure you will find your place doing something else in the Air Force." The hollow words slammed into my brain. It screamed, *I don't want to do something else.*

In the early phase of T-38 training, I had a young rookie instructor. Five of us were his first class. Curtis Crump in T-41s and Kent TeKrony in T-37s were never shy in pointing out my mistakes. Their effort paid off, and I graduated from those phases.

Now in T-38s, my instructor had little criticism. He was a nice guy. We were buds. But I missed essential skills, and three out of the four of us at his table failed the check ride, unable to successfully demonstrate the required maneuvers. Two of us failed completely out of the program.

The barrel roll did me in. I could not coordinate between the seat-of-the-pants feeling, the visual image through the windscreen, and the control and power needed.

As always in pilot training, the instruction moved quickly with little pause for the student who fell behind. Student pilots were dropped from the program in a heartbeat in the elim (elimination) ride.

Though everyone wished me well, Duke, another trainee who knew exactly how to approach the flying board I would face, was most helpful. He said, "Be insistent that you want to fly. Don't accuse anybody—just tell the facts. If they ask you if you want to make it a career, tell them you are open." Miraculously he had come alongside with the right guidance.

I waited for a few weeks for the board. I felt nervous and awkward. But when I stood before the four senior officers in a small paneled room, I told the facts without accusing my instructor. They decided to put me back in the program in the next class behind my original class, 68-E.

One of the things I learned in pilot training is that I am not a "stick," someone who is a natural where performance comes automatically and is executed brilliantly without thought. Though I became a very good pilot, it took study, work, and diligence.

Chuck Yeager was honored for having "the right stuff." The board guessed that I had it, and four successful years of flying operational aircraft proved them right.

Back In

H e would be the first to get the good news.

"Duke, I can't thank you enough. Your wise counsel on meeting the board saved me. It's a miracle. They really did listen to the facts. They restored me to the program."

His genuine smile showed that he shared my victory.

"Wow. I'm glad everything worked," he answered. "Well, you have your task cut out for you. Hope you get a good IP for the rest of training."

I still felt bad for the novice instructor. Would things work out for him in his career? I did not see him after the board, but a couple of men with the same name reached advanced rank in the Air Force.

The class I joined, 68-E, was one class behind my original class. It boiled with a fighter pilot mindset, a less civilized tone than my previous class. They had worked through two phases together and shared their own camaraderie and history.

Fred Olmstead, tall, lanky and athletic, became my IP. His perpetual impish grin said this was his world—he lived to fly. As an aggressive F-4 pilot, he later downed four MIGs in Vietnam. The History Channel recorded his dogfights and a copy of that program is in my library. His consistent, confident instruction enabled my steady progress.

Formation flying, though introduced earlier, now became a major phase of our training. I adjusted to the small control and power changes needed to fly rock-solid wing on a lead aircraft. That position was, "wingtip in the star, even with the tailpipe."

When Fred took me to that position for the first time, we kept approaching closer and closer.

My senses screamed *What are you doing? I can't do this. We are going to hit him.*

Afterwards Fred asked, "How did you feel when we got into position?"

"You guys are crazy. It feels like I am going to rip off his wing tip."

After mastering straight and level flight, turns in either direction gradually became steeper, always holding the wingman position. I had to remain in formation when pulling Gs or even inverted. On occasion, lead would waggle his wings, shaking me out to a more distant position, called "extended" or "extended formation."

After mastering flying as a wingman, I had to be the lead ship, first in a two-ship formation then in a four-ship. I learned to lead with smooth control and power changes, even in turns or pulling Gs, so my wing men could stay with me.

The deep inward satisfaction after formation flights said, *This I love.*

Lost and Found

"Wanna play Top Gun today?" my IP Fred asked before a training mission.

"You've got to be kidding," I replied, "What do we do?"

My IP was referring to the Fighter Weapons School of the Navy at Miramar Naval Air Station in San Diego, California.

"After takeoff, join up on me then follow me in trail," he replied.

Joining up was a delicate maneuver by which two aircraft that had taken off separately joined together as a two-ship formation.

Once I joined up with my instructor, what followed was the greatest workout I had ever experienced in formation.

In trail formation, I followed directly in back of him at perhaps seventy-five or one-hundred feet. I needed to be careful to stay below his tailpipe exhaust. If I ventured up into the exhaust stream, it would flip me out of control.

He did every maneuver in the book to lose me, pulling Gs, tight turns, inverted, negative Gs. It was great fun chasing each other in supersonic aircraft. It was like following another aircraft in a hostile situation, trying to gun him down. I never considered that Fred had the ability to lose me. But he was the instructor and vastly more experienced.

All of a sudden, he disappeared.

Where is he? My head swiveled in every direction: up, down, I rolled, climbed, dove, but I could not find him.

One moment he was there, another moment he wasn't. It happened so fast I did not even remember what maneuver lost me. I had to return to Reese humiliated as a "lost wingman." On reflection, I realized it was part of the training. They wanted to see if I would follow procedures even when lost from a formation.

The T-38 phase ended in a whirlwind of details. We took our civilian written examination for our commercial pilot's license. Because we had accumulated so many flying hours, there was no need to fly with a civilian flight examiner. The military process was more demanding.

In my deepening friendship with Beverly, questions gripped me as I finished pilot training: *Will I go to Vietnam? Will we be separated for a year? What aircraft will I get?*

I filled out my wish list, my preference for an operational assignment. We were nurtured in aggressiveness, so I applied for fighters first then for other aircraft. A few applied for anything that would keep them out of combat, particularly the family men. How close you came to your choices was all dependent upon class standing.

Proposal

If Bev says yes, should we get married before I go to Vietnam?

Our friendship grew during the end of pilot training. In either informal or formal social occasions, Beverly shone. She had great poise and maturity.

In some level of insanity in the fall of 1967, I suggested to Beverly that we date other people. I was unwilling to commit to a deeper relationship or marriage. Released from dating each other exclusively, she soon had a full dating docket. That burned me. Some of the guys interested were schemers. I've always contended that I rescued her from a dreadful fate—sleazy lowlife fraternity men.

Though she was only nineteen, the competition made me realize that if I didn't grab her quickly, I would lose her. We began dating more seriously. One December night, I said, "Tomorrow night we need to talk about something serious."

Because of uncertainties in my childhood, discussion of serious issues was not my strong suit. But I thought through our strong compatibility as a couple and had written down a number of observations. Looking to the future, I had written, "God is beginning a new chapter in our lives."

The central question that tormented me was *What if I am killed and she faces the heartbreak of having lost her husband, continuing on alone? Shouldn't we wait until I return?*

In the darkened parking lot in front of her dorm I asked, "Will you marry me?" I had no assurance at all that she would say yes.

"Yes," was her smiling, tearful answer.

Her answering immediately amazed me and filled me with joy. I had even brought the ring with me.

"Why wait?" Beverly shocked me by saying. "After the graduation ceremony, why don't we get married that evening?"

"Do you think you and your parents can pull off a wedding only ten weeks away?"

Together we decided, "Sure, there's lots of uncertainties. But let's take the leap."

Despite the short time available, Bev and her folks decided they had enough time to plan for the evening wedding.

We arranged a pre-marital counseling session with her pastor though I thought I knew everything there was to know about life and marriage. Now, as a pastor myself, I insist that all couples I marry have thorough counseling.

Although we anticipated the joy of marriage, we both felt the sledgehammer reality of separation. After leaving in May for Vietnam, we would have seven months apart. It seemed we would never be together again. But there was the distant glimmer: a five-day R & R, (rest and recuperation) in Hawaii.

My anticipated tour in Vietnam would allow her to complete her junior year at Texas Tech. Though we longed for her to graduate, that might have to wait.

WINGS GIVEN AND CLIPPED

etting my wings *Wow! What will it be like,* I daydreamed, envisioning the glowing silver treasure on my uniform.

"The assignments are in," a breathless classmate exhaled at the door of our training room.

I ran to my box in the mail room, ripped through the envelope, and read, "C-7A Caribou, 537th Tactical Airlift Squadron, Phu Cat, Vietnam." I rested against the wall, absorbing the news. Just as I figured, a one-year tour in Vietnam. *Caribou? What's that?*

The assignments came in time for them to be entered into my graduation book. Because of their high class standing, 10 percent got the coveted fighter assignment. The rest of us went to the supposedly despised "many motors," multi-engine aircraft. Despite our yapping about a fighter slot, I cannot recall anyone displeased with his assignment. More important than our destination was earning our cherished wings.

Going to the Caribou was almost perfect. In a sense, operational flying of the "Bou" in Vietnam would rely heavily on the brown bars—the second lieutenants. The squadron leadership would fly our backsides off.

In many ways, flying is learned by doing for hundreds or thousands of hours. I would learn a lot flying the Caribou.

Ninety-five percent of my class went to Vietnam.

Curious about my base, Phu Cat, I found it was near the port of Qui Nhon on the coast. Facts about the base and pictures emerged from the military newspaper, *Stars and Stripes*.

The morning of February 24, 1968, fifty-four of us in dress blues graduated in the base chapel. Seventy-eight had started a year before. Family crowded into the back. I received the coveted silver wings, and afterward, Beverly pinned them on with a kiss.

My mother, brother, and a sister flew out for the ceremony. They all knew it was a huge accomplishment. Though my dad had died in the previous months, I could envision his approving bear hug. Dad was always a hugger. I imagined his tearful, "Congratulations, Son." It was his victory, too.

That evening, Beverly and I were married at Crescent Park Baptist Church, her home church in Odessa, Texas, in the heart of the oil fields. The uncomplicated ceremony included my explanation that the Lord had changed our lives by faith in Him. I explained that we purposed to serve Him together, both in the Air Force and in life afterward. A punch and cake reception capped the ceremony.

Our honeymoon began with a drive to California. Being together on the road was heaven. Our marriage and successful completion of pilot training filled me with gratefulness.

But someone spoofed that I got my wings in the morning—and got them clipped at night.

Getting There

Dual Honeymoon

"Sorry, Son, we are short on housing. But there is a guy in Stone's River who rents apartments and trailers."

Heaven is being on your honeymoon with the love of your life and being a newly- commissioned Air Force pilot. I carried Beverly across the threshold of our temporary piece of the dream: our little silver trailer.

After graduation and wedding, our euphoria carried us west, lodging at economical transient housing at military bases. No frills, but cheap, clean, and comfortable.

We took in Disneyland then cruised up scenic, coastal US Route 1 and stayed in a cabin in the Redwoods. After a whistle stop in the Bay Area, we motored east to Sewart Air Force Base in Tennessee, near Nashville, for training in the C-7A.

Checking into my training unit, having earned my wings, eliminated the feeling of arriving as one of the herd. I now had an identity. No indignities, just right to the flying. No more pilot training IPs shouting, "Put your hands in your lap!"

Don, my instructor, welcomed me. "Hi Jon, great to have you here. Let's walk out to the airplane. I'm back from a year in-country [Vietnam]."

His year of experience would teach me much of what I needed to know—he had been there and done it. I hung on his every word.

Walking out to the airplane for the first time, my heart in my throat: *I am going to spend a year in this bird. What will it be like? Will I be able to make the transition?*

When I first encountered the airplane, twin ramps were down in back. We simply walked into it! *Is it possible for this huge monstrosity to fly?* The ramps enabled a small vehicle to drive right into the cargo hold. Up to now, I had flown smaller aircraft, but as I adjusted to the Caribou, the feel became natural. I came to love everything about this airplane. We were wed.

The pilot and co-pilot sat side by side, sometimes with a flight mechanic in a jump seat between us. I was accustomed to steering the aircraft with the rudder pedals. Now a wheel at the pilot's left hand directed nosewheel steering.

Don gave me important details. "What sets the Caribou apart from all other transports in Vietnam is short-field landings. Here at Sewart, you will land in a dirt strip, right in the middle of the field. We'll try it with full flaps but notice that you have greater control with partial flaps." I lived off his wise lesson for a year.

Honeymoon heaven could have lasted forever, but we quickly packed up and moved to our next stop—survival training.

Mutual Prisoners
of War

Bent low on my hands and knees, in my flight suit, in the inky blackness, I crawled across the dirt and rock of the Eastern Washington landscape. *"Ouch!"* I had crawled into thorn bushes. I rolled on my back and plucked out the thorns I could feel with my fingers. I heard an animal sound. *What kind of critters do they have out here?* Crawling again, I could smell the perspiration drenching my flight suit. Suddenly, shouts in a foreign language and a big hand on my collar raised me up. Pushed and manhandled toward a prisoner of war (POW) enclosure in an underground cave, I joined others also apprehended.

It was all part of a training simulation of combat conditions.

Along with all the aircrew flying over the jungles of Vietnam, I faced the challenge of crash landing or being shot down. Fighter crews faced the prospect of bailing out. In the jungle, I might have only what was in one of the pockets of my flight suit or what was strapped to me. In two phases, one in the States and one in the Philippines, fliers were prepared to survive in the jungle and even the dread prospect of being captured. The instructors tried to duplicate the stark realities of the POW experience such as the torture and interrogation at the "Hanoi Hilton." The motto of the unit conducting the training was "Return with Honor."

After Caribou school, Bev and I flew to Spokane, Washington, to experience the Stateside version of that training.

Beverly had her own challenge—a dingy, cut-rate motel near the base in thirty degree weather with little nearby. It was all we could find. It was her own POW ordeal. She wrote thank-you notes for wedding gifts, and I caught a ride back to the motel every few days.

With the training completed, we returned to Travis AFB for my flight to the Philippines. For guys headed to Vietnam, flights were in multiple segments. I took three commercial flights of five hours each leg to reach the Philippines. Packed in like cattle, with no leg room, we endured swirling cigarette smoke. At that time, smoking was still allowed on commercial flights—another survival experience.

Hardest of all was saying goodbye to Beverly, my bride of two-and-a-half months. We had been together in travel and training assignments. Now the question re-emerged, *Will we ever see each other again?* If I survived combat, we would next see each other at R & R. Though a comforting thought, the seven months wait seemed a lifetime.

PHONY E & E

I pried myself out of the sardine can and stepped onto the sweltering ramp at Clark Airbase, Philippines. Palm trees greeted my arrival in the tropics.

Shouldering my duffle bag, I picked my way through the terminal jammed with sleeping or sitting GIs to catch a bus to jungle survival training. Waiting outside, I found Taylor, a lieutenant, who had just finished the training.

"Jungle survival?" he asked.

"Yeah," I answered. "What's up in the training here?"

He answered, "Some interesting stuff about the jungle, but you won't get any sleep. The instruction in the heat is bearable, but the barracks aren't. No AC. Do they think this is the Stone Age? Then you go into the jungle for a couple of days. I slept on a bed made of branches. Major chiropractic damage. Then there's the one-night E & E (escape and evasion). You're supposed to sleep in a parachute hammock. I suffered all night."

The blue bus rolled up, and I thanked Taylor for his tips. Though Fairchild prepared us for the POW experience, Clark prepared us for survival in the jungle.

We pulled up to a white-fenced training area with a sign: "PACAF Jungle Survival School. The College of Jungle Knowledge. Learn and Return."

My class started the next day, but night in the stifling barracks only offered a worn ceiling fan for relief. Fortunately, the soft drinks were cheap, the equivalent of pennies in the US.

The headquarters of the 13th Air Force stood at the end of the mile-long parade field lined with orange-red flame trees. Rows of large homes of senior officers circled the huge rectangle.

The training prepared us for conditions in Vietnam, including a triple-canopy jungle, hidden pits with sharpened bamboo pungi stakes, and the challenge of avoiding capture. I learned to survive on what I found and to sleep on a bamboo platform.

In the final exercise, we attempted to run away from Negrito tribesmen, a largely futile attempt. They were fast and in their home territory. Three of us ran into the jungle and strung our parachute hammocks between trees. I carried five lives in the form of small paper chits which the tribesmen could trade for rice. I lost three of mine to worthy opponents when they found me. Fortunately, we did not fall off a cliff, whose edge we approached in the dark. That fate might have been less painful than the makeshift hammock.

Apart from the lack of sleep, I enjoyed the Philippines. I had no idea this was my future home. Three years of flying C-118 hospital ships out of Clark would follow my year at Phu Cat.

Into Vietnam

My gut knotted as we made our landfall in the delta of South Vietnam. This was it. *I'm in the war*, I admitted. Would we take ground fire or be shot down? Where were the blossoming ack-ack bursts like those in World War II B-17 movies? They sometimes said the flak was so thick you could walk on it.

Before the flight, having lived through jungle survival, I was back to the jungle of the Clark terminal, jammed with GIs draped everywhere. I endured the endless line, presented my orders, and waited for anything going to Tan Son Nhut Airport, Saigon, South Vietnam. It was the necessary entry point for my year "in country."

Two days of waiting concluded when I heard my name called in a list and caught a flight into Vietnam in a C-118. This four-engine military version of the DC-6 airliner was configured with seats facing backwards. *What's the deal with this? Don't they know which way we are going?* But this military version, in contrast to airliner seating, made more sense. In case of an accident or forced landing the passengers had back support. Eventually I would spend three years in this bird. Granted, it was older, but it had perhaps the most dependable prop engines ever made, the Pratt and Whitney R2800.

The country looked peaceful yet ominous. We entered at an altitude that ground fire could not reach. Though I didn't see airstrikes in progress, I could see craters in various places where conflict or airstrikes had occurred. The muddy brown delta of the Mekong River contrasted with the verdant rice paddies and dark green forests.

I had heard of the fighting around Saigon the previous February 1968, during "Big Tet." The North Vietnamese and Viet Cong used the national holiday as an occasion for a countrywide offensive, wagering that the general populace would join their cause.

My puzzlements and reflections were interrupted by a blast of tropical heat as we pulled up to the terminal, and the cargo doors were opened. Encumbered with my gear, I trudged to the terminal amidst the whine of jet engines and the sweet rush of JP-4 exhaust that distorted my sight.

Tan Son Nhut, the center of the war, was a conglomeration of the old and the new: clap-trap Quonset huts mixed with French-style buildings, weeds, and aircraft of every vintage.

At some point, it hit me. *I have an enemy out there who wants to kill me.* I struggled with this throughout my tour. *I am a nice guy. What is it they don't understand?* It made sense to my head but not my heart.

Tan Son Nhut

In my dreams of arrival, when I cracked the door of the terminal, a second lieutenant in a flight suit immediately ran over with a couple of other brown bars in flight suits. "Lieutenant Drury? We've been waiting for you. Jim, carry his duffel bag. There's our Bou right across the ramp. Let's go. We'll be in Phu Cat before you know it. You want to fly it?"

It didn't quite happen that way.

My duffel bag on my shoulder, I bucked the wind of jet exhaust and followed the stream of humanity through tropical heat to the terminal. There I encountered my next challenge. As the primary port-of-entry for Vietnam, a crowd of GIs waited in various lines for processing or flights. It seemed mass confusion. Though self-impressed with my rank, as my gold bars radiated brilliant amber light, nobody turned to notice. I was just a body waiting to be moved to some other part of the landscape. My disappointment and frustration growing, I stood in endless lines along with the humblest private. After over an hour, I was finally able to request a flight to Phu Cat. More waiting.

I found a ramshackle soda and food stand and bought a Coke. There was no seating, so I sat on the floor with my back against the wall. The Vietnamese in the Coke stand were the first ones I had seen. I had been told you could not tell the Viet Cong from the loyalists.

How about these people in the snack bar? They look suspicious to me. Will they throw a hand grenade when my back is turned? Are the Cokes poisoned?

I nodded off. From time to time, lists of names were read for different flights. Late in the day, I finally heard my name and caught a flight to a base close to mine, Qui Nhon.

My flight was a C-130 *Hercules*, a superb tactical supply bird but a miserable ride. In the red fabric troop seats, I could neither sit up nor lie down. They seemed designed by scheming back surgeons to generate a stream of screaming, desperate customers. The agony might have been lessened if there had been a pleasant view out of windows. But portholes were few and required twisting around to get even a tiny look outside. On the ground we fried, not only on the ramp in the tropical heat, but now we were encased in the passenger compartment during ground operation.

When we reached altitude the air conditioning cut in, and then we froze. I shivered with no coat, trying to sleep in my half-sitting position.

Qui Nhon RON (Remain Overnight)

Late in the day, I walked down the C-130 ramp at Qui Nhon, a port city in central Vietnam. Finally, I was only a short airplane ride from Phu Cat.

Directed to the Airlift Control Element (ALCE) office which controlled all air traffic, I explained my plight. To my request for a flight to Phu Cat they replied, "The Caribous are in here all day. But they are done for today. It's twilight. Sorry. None will be in till tomorrow."

I thought, *This cannot be*. So close, yet so far.

"Can't I get there by road, by a jeep, or something?"

"At night? The Viet Cong own that road at night. They often blow up the natural gas pipe that crosses the road. No person in their right mind would take you."

"How about transient housing?" I asked. Though it sounds like a flophouse for the homeless and indigent, in the States I had used it often, even on my honeymoon.

I was directed to a small, old house, bordered by a wall of razor wire. With room for a dozen or more men, the primitive, worn, sagging bunks and broken concrete floor shocked me. The stench of urine permeated the room, as the small, stained bathroom and shower in the next room had no door. A bare light bulb hung from the ceiling. No frills here! I began to appreciate the tremendous sacrifice of others in the military who endured these conditions or worse.

Army officers came and went all night, making sleep difficult. They caught what rest they could while making connections for transportation or troop movement. Some required the blinding bare light bulb to be turned on.

In the morning, I held my breath, endured a shower in the filthy bathroom, then tried to find coffee and breakfast. Showing mercy on a guy in a flight suit who looked lost, a Navy Lieutenant, J. G. took me in tow. He worked in the large harbor of Qui Nhon tracking ship and boat traffic through the port and offered me a tour. With semi-circular windows, his work station that tracked all the water traffic resembled a control tower at an airport. The Viet Cong and North Vietnamese moved many of their supplies by water.

He then led me to a large dining room with an uneven yellow linoleum floor where I was able to get coffee, bacon, and eggs. The Army and the Navy always proved to be good hosts, always faithful comrades in arms.

After coffee and breakfast, finally feeling human again, I set out to find a flight to Phu Cat.

UNEXPECTED BEAUTY

fter breakfast, I shouldered my green duffel bag and walked to the flight line to find a bird going to Phu Cat, hopefully a C-7A. I checked in with the ALCE and waited.

The Qui Nhon field teemed with the noise and exhaust of forklifts, jeeps, trucks, and French motorbikes. Around them swirled troops coming and going along with Vietnamese civilians. On the edge of the field, people living in wooden shipping containers shocked me. But from the dirt and squalor, I noticed young Vietnamese girls walking in their white *ao dais*, impeccably clean. Children on their way to school appeared clean, uniformed, and neat.

One of the rare treats of Qui Nhon, hard to find elsewhere, was a USO (United Service Organization) that served the soldiers. If you braved the line, you could buy a rare dish of ice cream or even a hamburger and French fries. They were an imprecise imitation of the stateside original but a treat nonetheless. We paid for our treasures with Military Payment Certificates (MPC), "funny money."

At the USO, you might see a creature who stunned the senses—a "round eye," an American female. All the guys shared the World War II sentiment, "There is nothing like a dame!"

The city's beautiful white beach became a haven for R & R, given to all the troops. Near the beach, I later visited a leper colony and admired the courage of its residents.

The ramp hosted a garden variety of smaller wartime aircraft such as Air Force O-2 observation planes and Army Beavers. The Beaver, also made by De Haviland like my Caribou, seemed a lumpy, ungainly monstrosity with a big radial engine, but then, it was not my aircraft.

I agonized through the morning, sitting on the edge of a bench, analyzing every aircraft coming in to land.

Finally, in late afternoon, one of the Phu Cat Caribous came in. It looked amazing and beautiful. I was able to hitch a ride back to Phu Cat. Though I was in an immense hurry to reach my base, the crew first had to load their cargo. The ramp bulged with palletized cargo of all sizes and shapes. Forklifts plied their trade with pallets of rice, ammunition, and rations.

Riding in the troop seats of a Caribou eclipsed my experience in the C-130. The seats, though the same red fabric and aluminum as the C-130, were much more comfortable. And the visibility was better since the windows were larger. I could see the line of hills to the west of Qui Nhon where I would later search for a downed flier.

As usual, the Caribou was the best of the best.

Phu Cat

Thousands of acres of luxuriant green rice fields stunned me when we were finally airborne for Phu Cat. Twenty miles long and ten miles wide, the plain of Binh Dinh Province, surrounded by hills, was called "the rice bowl of Vietnam." Small villages dotted the green with Vietnamese working the fields assisted by oxen. Later I would see one of my friends bail out of an F-100 into these rice paddies. From the air, I could see the blue South China Sea to the east, but on the ground, a range of hills blocked the view.

To strengthen the war effort, Phu Cat, eighteen miles north of Qui Nhon, was dropped into the rice bowl. Constructed from scratch in 1966 and 1967, at first the runway was 3,000 feet of dirt. The 459th and 537th Tactical Airlift Squadrons began operating there in January 1967. Then the Navy paved the runway, the horizontal part of the base, the 10,000-foot runway completed in March. In April, the 37th Tactical Fighter Wing arrived with its F-100s.

An Air Force Red Horse Squadron built the vertical part of the base: the buildings, barracks, and offices. The term *Red Horse* is the acronym for Rapid Engineer Deployable Heavy Operational Repair Squadron.

Fighters and larger, faster aircraft needed all of the 10,000-foot runway. Our Caribous, using only 700 feet or so for landing, needed only the average overrun at either end of the runway.

For me, joy of joys, Phu Cat was American, all-American. In everything from pancakes in the morning, doctors in white coats with stethoscopes, and basketball courts, we knew what to expect. An oasis for the American military had blossomed in Southeast Asia.

The familiar paradigm not only helped us live in the combat environment, but the familiarity helped us concentrate on the combat mission.

The flight line held not only our Caribous, but also fighters of different types including some of the National Guard. A view from the air showed rows of hangars and hard stands. The hard stands were heavy enclosures to protect aircraft against mortar and rocket fire or air attacks. Rows of louvered enlisted barracks blended with two-story officer barracks, mango trees, and grass. Here and there we could spot the foundations of former homes and wells.

I took comfort in the presence, next to Phu Cat, of ROK (Republic of Korea) troops. Known to be tough in combat, nobody messed with these guys, especially not the enemy. One of their pastimes was firing a 155mm howitzer for entertainment.

After months of training assignments and despite the combat environment, it would be good to settle in to Phu Cat, my home for a year.

Pilot Training T-41 solo   Reese AFB, pilot training room

Supersonic T-38 *Talon*

Wings and Rings! Jon receives wings, married to Beverly the same day.

Operations Building, Phu Cat, Vietnam

Phu Cat officer's quarters

Jon and his C-7A Caribou   Caribou operations, Pleiku, Vietnam

Pleiku loading ramp

Cruising at 105 knots (Copyright © 2003 Bob Dugan)

Christmas Santa Bou (Copyright © 2012 Jerry Presley)

Flat tire at Dak Seang

Forklift loading "Where are you taking me?"
(Copyright © Al Cunliffe)

Ambulance and Phu Cat civilian dispensary

Kids at school construction project

Jon and Glenn Helterbran at civic action event

Pastor and kids at Phu Cat church

The kids were great

Elephant wrapped for transport (C-7A
Caribou Association)

Jon after Caribou days

HUMBLE COPILOT

WELCOME tO tHE 537th

A t last I walked down the airplane ramp at Phu Cat, my assigned base.³ Jake, the aircraft commander said, "If you wait for us to complete our paperwork, you can ride back in with us. Your unit, the 537th, is right next to ours."

I could not accept his charitable offer. I was not part of their unit. *Is the 537th helpless to pick up their own pilots?* It may be hard for those not in the military to understand the pride each man takes in his unit.

I walked to base operations. The duty officer in green, sweat-stained fatigues sat behind a counter. "I am a new pilot for the 537th TAS, one of the Caribou outfits. Can I call my unit?" I requested.

Before long, a blue truck with a big cab and a truck bed drove up. I threw my gear in the back, and I questioned the 537th duty officer as we pulled away. "What is this thing? It's not a passenger car, and it's not a truck."

"It's a six-pax." We can put six crew members in the cab and all their gear in back."

We pulled up to the squadron building, a plain two-story olive drab and gray building on the flight line. When I walked into the squadron, the on-duty operations officer said, "Welcome, Drury. Reach into the fridge in the lounge and grab a soda. Good to have you here. Just don't plunder the fridge too often. That stuff is hard to get hold of."

The ice-cold Pepsi was the best thing I had tasted in a couple of days.

He assigned me to a barracks room on the second floor in the housing area, and the duty officer took me to my room.

Soon after my arrival, I had to see the guy with the stethoscope. The Philippine jungle had given me a bad case of something similar to poison oak on my arms and hands. When I saw the doc, I asked him, "What is it?"

He returned the question by asking, "What is it?" He explained that outside of the States, we know little of the plants and bugs in the tropics and gave me some calamine lotion. I repeatedly painted the stuff on my creeping crud, and slowly it made some headway in drying up the infection.

Though somewhat diseased, I had arrived and looked forward to my copilot checkout. *I wonder what kind of instructor pilot I am going to get. Maybe another who shouts, "Put your hands in your lap!"*

READY, SET, FLY

Our two-story squadron building held the nerve center of our operation. Inside the front door, the hall to the left led to the operations desk. A chalk board on the wall summarized the nine or ten missions for the day. We received our mission assignments there at the operations desk—a ten-foot counter with the operations staff on the other side. This was where I would receive my first Aircraft Commander mission months later, a mid-day jaunt to our shortest strip, 1,100-foot Plei Me, on an urgent supply mission.

The connecting lounge next door with an enemy AK-47 mounted on a beam, had little use despite the soft leatherette chairs. Few flight crews had time to lounge. You might try to study there, but likely someone would ask you to run an errand since you obviously had nothing to do. It did, however, hold a treasure in Southeast Asia (SEA), the locker of cold sodas.

An outside stairway led to a larger meeting room upstairs that every few months hosted a Squadron Commander's Call. All the flying officers then gathered for update, instruction, or reproof. Down the hall from the meeting room, offices housed those with duties in addition to flying such as Awards and Decorations, Training, and Standardization/ Evaluation. Brown bars, second lieutenants like me, did not receive such extra duties. We were new to all aspects of an operational assignment. Instead, they flew our pants off.

At the back of the operations desk a door opened to a Command Post (CP) shack heavily protected with sand bags in case of attack. It stood between the two Caribou squadrons, like the middle bar of an H, and held radios that kept us in communication twenty-four hours a day. At night, we rotated, staffing the CP with the other squadron, the 459th.

At the squadron before each mission launch, we checked out a Smith & Wesson (S & W) .38 handgun, holster, and belt, along with our flak jacket. We stowed the .38s and the bulky jackets in back of the bulkhead (aluminum wall) at the front of the cargo compartment. If flying over an area especially prone to ground fire, some guys stuffed the flak jackets under the pilot and copilot seats for protection.

Every morning, we picked up a black briefcase kit containing all the forms necessary for our flight. The forms, completed at the end of the day, summarized our loads and flights and anything that needed to be reported to command or maintenance. Once fully encumbered with all the gear, we rode to our assigned Caribou in the six-pax, unloaded, and readied the aircraft for the mission.

Phu Cat Digs

At the housing area, I grabbed my gear out of the back of the six-pax and walked to a gray, two-story wooden barracks. My room on the second floor was twelve by twelve. A country boy I once knew would have said, "This room ain't big enough to whup a dog in!"

A bunkbed lined up on the left, and straight ahead stood a built-in shelf and desk made of plywood. I chose the lower bunk, but no one ever occupied the upper one. Though our rooms were small, we each had our own.

Each pair of rooms shared an air conditioner, an accommodation to the pilot's need for rest between missions. I tried studying at the desk, but it was too claustrophobic. So I used the squadron lounge, the library, or even the Officer's Club.

With other pilots, I shared a large common bathroom and shower with a cement floor.

A Vietnamese "hooch" maid came twice a week to gather laundry and replace the sheets. Some of the hooch maids chewed betel nut, which stained their mouths brownish-red. It supposedly gave a rush equivalent to six cups of coffee, but tragically it also led to an early grave.

"Go to the bunker. Mortar attack!"

When mortar rounds hit the base one night, sirens wailed. The person first to hear them banged on our doors. I pulled on some clothes and ran to the bunker at the end of the barracks. Habitable only by sewer rats, the small, miserable sand-and-dirt tunnel had only enough head room for me to sit on the ground or stand hunched over.

When they banged on his door, one pilot hollered, "I'm staying in bed. Charlie [nickname for the Viet Cong] is not going to hit me."

We agonized, waiting for the all clear, which came after an hour or two. One guy found the fins from one of the mortar shells. The guy who slept through the raid was proven right, while the rest of us tried to straighten out sore backs.

For peaceful moments, a couple of banana loungers lay in the sun for those who wanted a tan. We limited our exposure due to the intensity of the Asian sun. Often I studied while getting a tan.

Early in the tour, a mouse came and went as he pleased in my room and always left calling cards. One day I found him dead. Could my dirty socks have spelled his doom.

THE CARIBOU

"**S**teep approach, wide angle cockpit visibility and excellent control at low approach speeds enable the pilot to pick with precision the point on the strip for touch-down. Ultra short landing roll coupled with the long-stroke, rugged landing gear, makes year-round operation possible from unimproved thousand-foot jungle, bush or desert landing strips."

The description of the Caribou came from a November 1962 sales brochure by De Havilland, the plane's maker.[4] It was marketed in the early '60s as the DHC-4A. The US Army purchased the plane to support its new airmobile concept, and an Army Caribou company deployed to South Vietnam in the spring of 1962. By 1966, they had expanded to six companies directed by Army corps and division command.

In late 1965, the Army and Air Force Chiefs of Staff began discussions on the transfer of the Caribou to the Air Force. In April of 1966, they agreed to transfer the Caribous to the Air Force.

Later that year, Air Force air and ground crewmen began arriving in South Vietnam and were attached to the Army Aviation Companies to begin the transition. On January 1, 1967, the assets of the six Army companies were transferred to six Air Force squadrons. Two squadrons were activated at Cam Ranh Bay, two at Phu Cat, and two at Vung Tau. Vung Tau remained an Army airfield.

The Caribou was designated the USAF C-7A.

The small carrying capacity of the Caribou was at first considered a drawback by the Air Force. But its excellent maneuverability for short takeoff and landing, and airdrops in forward combat locations, provided the tradeoff. Simplicity of construction minimized the C-7A's vulnerability to ground fire.

The Air Force reactivated the 483rd Troop Carrier Wing (changed to Tactical Airlift Wing 1 August 1967) to direct the Caribou operation, and based it at Cam Ranh Bay. The six new squadrons each had sixteen Caribous and twenty-four aircrews, manning of 1,555 (including maintenance), replacing the 1,443 spots used by the Army Caribou units. The Army desired that the Caribous stay near enough to Army maneuver units to retain needed support. The Air Force continued to move toward central Air Force control. Finally, Defense Secretary McNamara ruled that the Caribous would be stationed at Air Force, not Army bases. Two squadrons each were then deployed to Cam Ranh, Vung Tau, and Phu Cat.[5]

Now the "Steep approach, control at low approach speeds, and short landing roll" belonged to the flyboys.

COPILOT CHECKOUT

"Hi, Jon. I'm Aubray Abrams. Great to have you here. I'll be the IP for your checkout. How was your trek from Tan Son Nhut?"

The personable, smiling captain met me in the corridor of the barracks.

"Apart from one night in the armpit of the world, reasonable," I answered.

"We fly together tomorrow. Can you meet me at 0500 hours in the chow hall, and I'll give you details on launching our mission tomorrow?"

Till now, my five military assignments had been training units. They were preparation, pretending, and practice. This was different. Now in an operational unit, everyone was busy, professional and focused, but busy. The air was different.

In the morning, Captain Abrams and I, in our flight suits, sat across each other over plates of scrambled eggs and coffee.

"From here we will catch a ride to the squadron in the six-pax. At the squadron, everything happens at once. We get our frag, which is a fragmentary flying order. I'll show you where to pick up your flak jacket and .38 S & W. Not many guys wear them. Most stow them in the front of the airplane."

Our mission call sign was Soul 03. Since all our missions were preparing for launch, initially we could not buck the line at the operations desk to learn our mission.

One of the operations staff spotted me and hollered, "Drury, you're new. Have you read the intelligence file?"

"I'm leaving on my first mission. Can I catch it later?"

"OK, do it in the next couple of days."

Aubray explained, "The frag describes what we are doing all day. Important details will either be in the frag or operations will spell it out such as a base under fire or a ton of heavy cargo."

Once in the air, he continued, "Today we have one of the milk runs, ferrying troops north from An Khe to the 1st Air Cavalry base at Camp Evans. Half our missions start this way. The second half of the day we do anything ALCE gives us."

At An Khe, we found a mass of newly arrived troops lined up for flights to Camp Evans. Captain Abrams explained, "We can take seventeen to twenty-two troops. Compared to a C-130 or C-123, that's small, but we get into much smaller strips than either of the other birds."

Learning everything at once set me pouring over manuals and procedures. I reveled in learning my aircraft and my mission. Aubray Abrams' comradeship contrasted with the intimidation of pilot training. Abrams brought out the best in me.

Could I measure up?

Air Cavalry

It felt good to have my first load on my first combat mission. The twenty newly arrived troops in combat gear wore the triangular 1st Cavalry Division (Airmobile) horse patch on their shoulders. I could not quench the tide of reality that they were headed for fierce jungle combat. They had a tougher role than I did.

Will I later carry some of these guys back in body bags?

We took off from An Khe to the south and turned, climbing around Hon Con Mountain, affectionately called "Hong Kong Mountain." The scars of tragic aircraft and helicopter crashes could be seen on the peak which jutted out of the landscape. Some had paid the price of flying near An Khe in poor visibility, fog or rain, perhaps trying to find the runway.

We leveled at 4,000 feet, flew northeast across a beautiful river and deep valley with rugged terrain, and crossed the former Bong Son airstrip and Landing Zone (LZ) Pony where some of our veteran pilots had shuttled before my time in what they called the "Bong Son Bounce."

At the South China Sea we went "feet wet" and turned north, up the coast. For a while, we were out of the range of ground fire and artillery.

Our run up the coast took us past Chu Lai, the Marine base, Da Nang, which could take the largest aircraft, and Hue, the old provincial capital.

Ten clicks (kilometers) away from Camp Evans, we turned inland and called the Evans tower. Our morning run took the troops to what looked like the armpit of the world. A small, primitive tarred ramp was tacked onto a bleak expanse of tents and temporary buildings. It was the northern basecamp for the Cav. The old cavalry used horses. The new airmobile Army used helicopters to insert troops into the battle zone. The Cav was known for air assault and tough combat.

In the summer of 1965, President Johnson beefed up the war by sending the Cav to the Ia Drang Valley for a major dogfight. Troops lifted into combat by Huey helicopters dropped into temporary LZs. Despite brutal, costly combat, the Cav drove back the North Vietnamese enemy.

We respected the Cav. I knew Neal, one of the pilots from the "First of the Ninth" of the Cav (1st Squadron, 9th Cavalry), notorious for their aggressiveness. One of their strategies was to hover over the enemy in a little Loach (LOH—Light Observation Helicopter), seeking to draw ground fire. Pinpointing their location, the enemy was then eliminated. Neal was shot down five times in one day and rescued each time. His courage and persistence awed me.

FLIGHT GLOVES

n the heat and dust, I trudged uphill from the flight line to a big corrugated metal building. The wooden door creaked as I entered. Inside, only the sound of the flies broke the silence of the airless, sweltering, and narrow lobby. My stifling Nomex flight suit, regulation for pilots, multiplied my misery. I rang the bell.

Nothing.

Why don't they air condition this sweat box?

After an initial polite wait, frustration growing, I hollered, "Anybody home?" Air Force Supply had many charms.

I came for desperately needed flight gloves. I flew two days out of three, and my treasured deerskin gloves deteriorated quickly as I handled cargo and worked in the cockpit. When the gloves contacted oil or gas, they absorbed it, degrading the palm of the gloves. Sometimes we had to refuel our own birds. All that wear left my gloves in shreds.

A supply troop with a protruding belly emerged and asked what I wanted. "I'm a pilot with the 537th and need replacement flight gloves." I showed him my tattered pair.

"Fill out this requisition form!" he barked, irritated at the interruption of his day. "You can't get anything without a requisition form."

"I already filled out the form," I barked back, my complexion reddening. "I left it here two weeks ago."

"What's your name?" I gave him my name and he disappeared into shelves filled with clothing.

During my year at Phu Cat, I had to replace my boots only once, but gloves were another story. If it had just been flying, such as I do now, there would be little wear. I've had the same pair for years, but the heavy wear inflicted by flying and loading almost daily in Vietnam deteriorated gloves fast.

"There's no record of your form. Better fill out another one." Repressing my frustration, I explained how badly I needed the gloves.

How could they lose track of my cotton pickin' form? I fumed to myself. *What if I lost track of my frag during a mission and told Colonel Wolfe I lost it? He might rip the wings off my flight suit!*

I completed the new form and asked, "How soon will they be in?"

He answered, "Check with us in a few weeks."

I couldn't wait a few weeks to fly, so I continued to aviate with the torn pair. Finally, after two or three tries—and time—my gloves came in.

In three months, I again trudged up the hill, tattered gloves in hand.

Wanna Race?

One hundred twenty knots—that was our number. We joked that the Caribou did everything at 120 knots: climb, cruise, and descend. Unhurried compared to other transports, we had barn doors hanging out in the wind. Our airfoils, the curved surfaces that give lift—wings and horizontal stabilizers—were sizeable.

One morning during my checkout, Aubray and I climbed out of An Khe at 120 knots with our full load of troops for Camp Evans. We leveled at the same airspeed for our run down the coast. Cruising peacefully, I dug in my flight suit pockets for maps and my handwritten frequency book, and I reviewed artillery sites inland. Artillery fire bases were always changing, and I scrambled to remember their location. Though unintended, friendly artillery could blow you out of the sky.

Suddenly, an Air America C-46 in the original unpainted aluminum pulled even with my copilot seat on the right. Though some Air America birds were marked, this was just a pure aluminum torpedo, a silver cigar.

He was too close for large aircraft, fifteen to twenty feet between wingtips. *What is up with this?* I wondered. Was the pilot having engine problems? Did he need an escort?

Aubray provided insight. "These guys are hot dogs. You never know what they're going to do."

The C-46 Commando, produced from 1940 to1945, was at the time the largest twin-engine transport in the world. Though over 3,000 were built, it was always overshadowed by its more numerous sister, the C-47 or DC-3, of which over 10,000 were built.

The Air America operation, covertly owned by the US government, conducted non-combat operations with over eighty planes and helicopters and over 300 pilots.

The C-46 pilot looked across to me from his cockpit, then, to my shock, shut down his left, number one, engine and feathered the prop, turning the blades into the wind. He advanced his right engine, number two, accelerated, and passed us. He was faster on one engine than we were on two. He might as well have shouted, "I'm hot; you're not! You're flying a dog. Hey, look at me!"

Perhaps he was asking, "Wanna race?" If so, we had lost out of the gate. Not built for speed, the Bou's specialty was short field landings. His cruise speed of 150 knots reflected his bigger engines, R-2800s as opposed to our R-2000s. The Caribou designers did not have sleek and sporty in mind. We just let the hot dog go and score his gotcha!

But we had our own gotcha! The C-46 could never get into the Plei Me runway of 1,100 feet of dirt. What we did, we did well.[6]

SWEat Out

Sometimes on the way to junior college in Charlie Dove's car, someone would holler, "Sweat out!" We rolled up the windows of the car and turned on the heater full blast to see who would chicken out first.

A Nomex flight suit was a Vietnam sweat out.

A flight suit is a full-body garment, similar to a jumpsuit worn by military aviators. It was made to be practical with loads of pockets and zippers. Flying missions in Vietnam, we lived in our flight suit. The Nomex fire retardant suit had been substituted for the old gray flight suit, which was thinner and more comfortable in hot weather. Though we knew about the fire-retardant qualities of the suit, in the tropical weather of Southeast Asia, we suffered interminably. We knew that the heavier fabric would protect the skin in case of fire. It seemed distant comfort in our suffering.

Often it was only when we leveled out at altitude after takeoff that we could cool off and get some air. Then windows on the side of the cockpit sucked in a cooling flow.

We wore our set of dog tags around our neck tucked inside the zipper at the top of the suit along with a P-38 folding can opener to open C ration cans. In pilot training, some wore a silk scarf, but in Vietnam few wore it because of the heat. High on my left sleeve in the two small, deep pockets, I carried a pen and a small flashlight.

In one of the front leg pockets of the flight suit, I kept a small white book with all the radio frequencies I needed in flight, including artillery frequencies. In another small, thin upper-leg pocket, I kept a pocket knife on a string which could be withdrawn quickly. The knife, useful for aviators who bailed out and needed to cut parachute shroud lines, helped me in loading. In one of the lower-leg pockets, I kept maps of areas of Vietnam, including detailed maps of smaller areas where I had marked artillery fire bases.

In one of the breast pockets of my flight suit, I kept my wallet, MPC funny money; in the other I kept a New Testament and Psalms someone had given me.

The New Testament's location duplicated what men of other ages called a "Heart Shield Bible." My father-in-law, Edward Porter, carried a copper-covered New Testament over his heart in the Battle of the Bulge with the 84th Infantry Division. The testament was inscribed by his mother.

Though the Nomex suit was a sweat out, it was home and had everything I needed for flying.

Civic Action

Stateside reports depicted the suffering of the South Vietnamese people in the multiple tragedies of warfare. Now, in close proximity, I experienced pangs of conscience. *Isn't there something I can do for the people of Vietnam, beyond military duties?* I learned that the US military performed "civic action" to benefit the local population. Curious, I queried a tall, senior Southern Baptist chaplain in fatigues.

"The term *civic action* is used when service personnel give time and resources apart from their duties to help the Vietnamese. It spreads good will," he explained.

"Where and when does this happen?" I asked.

"The civilian civic action officer has an office on base. Why don't you sit down with him to get the picture?"

My knock on the small office produced Dave, a busy, thirty-ish guy with dark hair, in an office jammed with files and papers. Ready to leave, he said, "Ride with me, and I will fill you in."

In his jeep, we zigzagged through the gate of Phu Cat, protected by barbed wire and guard towers, turned right on the main highway, and wheeled through trees and lush green rice paddies.

"In every case, Vietnamese leaders decide what needs to be done, and we coordinate proposed projects with base commanders and chaplains."

We stopped to talk plans with Troung and Pham, sixty-ish Vietnamese provincial leaders in traditional clothing of printed cloth. Their wisdom and demeanor impressed me, though I knew nothing of the projects they discussed.

On one occasion, men at Phu Cat assembled health kits in brown cardboard boxes for school children. They took them by truck to Dap Da, a small church and school, twenty minutes from our base. A small, gabled wooden building doubled for both purposes. No comfy church pews here; wood benches provided the seating.

Stateside schools dwarfed this one of fifty children, but the young students in their neat uniforms charmed us with their shy smiles. The jet-black-haired pastor could not have weighed more than a hundred pounds, but he impressed me with his gracious character.

We had firearms and green flak jackets in case of trouble. We looked dangerous, but Air Force guys with firearms are probably a greater danger to themselves than to the enemy. In one unit, a man had tried a western quick draw and shot himself in the foot.

In another project, we helped build a village school of framing and plywood. Some GIs had actual building skills to contribute. Having been a hod carrier toting bricks at a construction site at home, I carried supplies for the guys doing productive work.

Civic action would soon lead me to drive an ambulance, my most satisfying contribution.

Ambulance Driver

"**W**ould you like to drive that thing?"

Dave, the civic action officer, took me to see a boxy, jeep-type ambulance at the base hospital. A small, white clinic was being built of framing and plywood in front of the main gate. The hospital was initiating limited free medical care for the Vietnamese residents of the village. Medical Civic Action Program (MEDCAP) clinics had been offering care to the Vietnamese as early as 1965.

The Vietnamese people lined up to receive outpatient care during the part-time hours. Though some came, I puzzled: *With free care, why is this place not mobbed?* Most of the Vietnamese seemed busy with farming. There also may have been a danger in identifying with the US troops.

Though thankful that the ambulance was a more active way to help the Vietnamese, I puzzled, *How am I going to find drivers for the days I fly?* Delegation was not my strong suit. I was more of a loner. I chose to ask the quiet guys with solid character to be my substitute.

The vehicle, painted white or green with a red cross on the side, may have been an M-725 Kaiser Jeep, off the production line in 1967 was most often seen in olive drab. It had bench seats inside but could also hold litter patients. Our short driving route passed through the zigzag barricade at the gate meant to deter car or truck bombs.

When patients treated at the clinic needed tests or medication available at the hospital, our ambulance came into play. We were the ride back and forth.

The patients entered the side door of the hospital, the entrance closest to the clinic. When I dropped them off at the hospital, I often escorted them out of the ninety-degree tropical heat into the air-conditioned comfort and antiseptic floors of the hospital.

Some of the Vietnamese, cut or injured working in the fields, were treated and bound with clean bandages. They often continued planting and returned with bandages caked with mud. The rice harvest and farming was their life. The doctor would again have to clean, treat, and wrap the injury.

I doubt that the doctors, nurses, or patients knew that the drivers were pilots and officers. Curry Taylor, Glenn Helterbran, and my IP, Aubray Abrams, were three who volunteered. I have since talked to others who drove but regret I have forgotten most of the names and have no list. I received great help. Thanks to all who took the time to drive and offer healing to the Vietnamese patients.[7]

Feather Number Two

"Feather number two," Mac, my aircraft commander, said. Because he caught me by surprise, and I had not picked up the clues as fast as he had, I am sure I blurted, "Huh?" in response to his request.

Though I would delight to relate my prowess as a copilot, I have more memories of my gaffes. Early in my year, I was flying with Mac as my Aircraft Commander. Flying feet wet near Chu Lai, engine number two, the right engine, suddenly began making mechanical noise, metal banging on metal. A fluctuating RPM gauge showed Mac the problem was the right engine

There was no previous warning of problems with that engine, but on occasion engines suddenly fail. Later a friend would have an engine failure in which fire streamed back from the deteriorating engine. The fire bottle discharged in the engine proved ineffective.

After shutting off the fuel and spark to the engine, Mac said, "Feather number two!" to me, his copilot. Feathering the prop turns the blades of the prop streamlined into the wind so the engine can cease motion. Allowing a bad engine to turn and receive fuel risks the danger of a fire.

Allowing a prop to windmill without power and without being feathered is a drag that slows the aircraft. In the adrenalin rush of mechanical problems, pilots have been known to feather the wrong engine.

I had never feathered an engine before, though the feather button was right above me. I moved too slowly, and after a few seconds, he said, "I guess I'll do it myself," which he did.

In a twin-engine aircraft, single engine procedures—flying with one engine out—offers the greatest challenge. On this occasion, being at altitude, the left engine needed minimal power, and several landing options simplified our need for a safe landing.

We made an emergency landing at Chu Lai and told the ALCE what had happened. We waited until later in the day when we could ride back with one of our Phu Cat Caribous.

An engine would have to be flown to Chu Lai with an engine change team.

Most pilots fly hundreds or thousands of hours before an emergency hits. Handling it takes knowledge of procedures, practice, and cool, steady thinking and action. Mac showed me that cool-headedness.

PILOt TEamWORK

Flying as a humble copilot often meant being subject to the egos of pilots who needed to prove they were god of the skies. Their inflated view of themselves could even damage their judgment. One of these Caesars, a major, drove me through a huge thunderstorm in Japan. Of course, he felt fearless and indestructible—his clouded view of himself.

Sadly, airplanes sometimes simply disappear in massive storms.

He never asked for my input and lost the benefit of teamwork that uses the skills and wisdom of the other pilot in the cockpit.

On the other end of the ego scale, I enjoyed flying with Captain George Kulik, one of our quiet, easygoing Aircraft Commanders. He was humble and professional. Once, I flew as his copilot at Camp Evans where we taxied out for takeoff. He chose a minimum ground roll takeoff on a rough runway to reduce wear on our tires. As copilot, I had the job of lowering twenty-five degrees of wing flaps. When ready to roll, Kulik applied full power—the sound of 10,000 hammers on a tin sheet. It was the signature sound of the Caribou. Moving the control column full back until rotation, he released brakes. We rolled and rolled and rolled and finally mushed into the air before the end of the runway. Kulik knew by the feel and length of the takeoff that I had missed the checklist item of flaps.

Normally, after liftoff the pilot raises the landing gear then gives the flaps-up command to the copilot. In this case, after raising the gear, he looked at the flap indicator to confirm I had never lowered the flaps.

"I guess you forgot to lower the flaps!" That was all he said. It was a casual but concerned comment. He didn't scream at me like a pilot training IP, but it might have been better if he had. Inwardly, I was screaming at myself. *You idiot! You idiot! What if we had crashed? It would have been your fault.*

Ouch! My red face and silence confirmed my failure. On a more critical strip it could have meant damage or disaster. It reminded me of one of my grade school teachers who accused me of not paying attention as I was constantly daydreaming and staring out the window.

Normally, in the cockpit there was an effective partnership, each respecting the role and opinion of the other. In flying, as in life, teamwork brings effectiveness and success.

My moral crisis grieved me for weeks.[8]

Handlebar Hijinks

Though the 537th was not a rebellious outfit, pilots exhibited individuality, fun, and adventure. It remains so today at reunions of Caribou aviators. One of our personalities was Charlie Tost, sporting a long red handlebar moustache. Though his 'stache did not violate regulations, it was not the clean-cut pilot look our superiors wanted. But Charlie was going to do what Charlie wanted to do. And so were we. We younger pilots decided to imitate Charlie. Of course, nobody in the command structure of the squadron joined in the idiocy. I have 8mm movies of the cockpit on one occasion, flying a mission, as we two pilots twirled our handlebars for posterity.

Back at Texas Tech, at great sacrifice, Beverly labored over her typewriter, cranking out term papers and theses, to afford $40 to send me a beautiful portrait of herself. When the studio portrait arrived, I was touched by her gift. The picture became the centerpiece of my postage stamp-sized room. Her portrait and letters were my great comfort in a long year. At times I felt, *I don't think I have ever been anyplace else. I have always been here and will always be here.*

Proud of my new facial hair, I sent my beloved a photo of myself with the 'stache. She cried, something I would never have anticipated. The guy in the picture was not the man she had married. We have since laughed about it, but she wrote at the time that I had done it to spite her. Actually, I had nothing to spite her for. She was a doll and still is. It was just comradery with my crazy outfit.

Always up to something, Charlie once said to our straight-laced, by-the-book, graying commander, "I am thinking about becoming a conscientious objector!" The declaration caught our leader by surprise as he and our unit would instantly become a leprous pariah.

He blurted out something like, "Why you son of a _____!"

Charlie retorted, "Just kidding!" That was Charlie.

On one occasion, Charlie engaged in a mutual dare with other junior pilots to shave their heads bald. The others chickened out, fearing the ire of our senior officers. But Charlie went through with it though of course he kept his long red handlebar.

I had never forgotten the fun Charlie injected into the 537th. Many years later, I met Charlie again in a strange situation. It was he who introduced me to the Caribou Association. But more of that later.

Thanks, Charlie.[9]

Command Post

"**D**rury. You've got command post duty Tuesday night. Don't forget."

What have I done to deserve this?

One boring duty of Caribou line pilots was manning the command post at night. When our turn came, every month or so, we hated it. The command post, shielded completely by sandbags, stood between the two Caribou squadrons, the 537th and the 459th. The building housed a long circular line of radios, telephones, and intercoms to keep both squadrons in communication twenty-four hours a day. In theory, it was a good opportunity to read and study, but by the end of the day, exhaustion clawed at us.

You had to barter with the other man on duty for time to sleep. Since there were two of us on duty, one from the 537th and one from the 459th, one stayed alert for radio, land line calls, or messages. *Alert* is a relative term because trying to stay awake was agony. We received few calls and messages.

The guy not on duty could sleep in the "hot bunk" where everyone slept. The bunk was a vintage folding military frame bed with springs and a thin gray mattress, undoubtedly a remnant of the Boer War. Though it was objectionable to the senses and a risk for communicable diseases, we were desperate for sleep. The one who stayed awake vowed to pick up the calls and messages for the one sleeping.

Classified messages came periodically and had to be picked up at an intelligence headquarters. To pick up the message, I thought I would walk into an office. But, since I was way down on the security pecking order (I never received a top secret clearance), I had to bend down and talk into a box or into a slit in a door. From the beginning of the through-the-slit communication, I was highly suspect. They evidently thought I was Ho Chi Minh in person, scheming to steal their precious information. I wondered, *Why do you let me fly your airplanes if you don't trust me?*

One night, I slept in my rotation when the 459th representative said he would pick up my messages, which he forgot to do. After serving my shift, I heard that Colonel Richardson, our Operations Officer, wanted to see me immediately. Irritated, he said I had failed to pick up a classified message during my night duty.

I told him, "The 459th guy said he would pick up my messages."

He thundered back "It was your responsibility!"

I heard that reproof more than once from a senior officer, and some of them could breathe fire. I could not fault Colonel Richardson. He was a straight-arrow professional and one of the men I most respected.

Autorotation

Our Caribou sat on the irregular gravel and tar that Camp Evans called a ramp, next to the runway.

Suddenly, everything came unglued as a chopper pilot hollered into the mike on tower frequency.

"Tower this is Dustoff One-Three, three clicks south. I have a big-time fire light and smoke in the cockpit. I need an autorotation to Runway Three-Six right now. Please clear all traffic." Dustoffs were the Army UH-1 Huey rescue helicopters. This one was three kilometers south of Camp Evans.

In a helicopter autorotation, the main engine is disconnected from the rotor system and the rotor is driven solely by the upward flow of air through the blades. Usually the engine has failed. The rotor acts as a huge parachute. To keep the proper airspeed, the approach is made at a fairly steep angle, requiring good pilot skills.

"Dustoff One-Three, Roger. Continue autorotation to Runway Three Six. What is your condition?"

"Dustoff has one WIA [wounded in action] and six souls on board. Fuel is half."

"Soul Four-Oh-Two [Caribou in the pattern] break out of the pattern for an aircraft emergency, runway unavailable. Soul Four-Oh-Four [us] do not taxi to the runway. Maintain your position till emergency is over." Actually, we didn't have our load yet and weren't going anywhere.

"Dustoff One-Three, the whole runway is yours."

In contrast to Air Force runways, no fire truck was provided for aircraft emergencies as I recall. You were on your own.

The autorotation landing of the Huey could best be described as a pancake with a couple of bounces, followed by a short scrape down the flexible aluminum runway. The pilots in olive-drab flight suits and grunts in fatigues leapt and crawled out of the chopper, the pilots grabbing at cords and flinging off seatbelts. All dove into the ditch beside the runway, anywhere away from the coming fire and explosion. The wounded soldier couldn't climb out. A crew member went back, grabbed him, then dragged him to the ditch with what little help the wounded man could give.

We expected to see fire or explosion any moment. If there had been one, we could have been torched also. We were close. Events happened too quickly to move our aircraft. The chopper did not catch fire, the engine began to cool, and eventually the chopper was moved, again opening the runway.

The helicopter pilot had done a sterling job on an autorotation, keeping his cool and landing safely. The first principle in a flight emergency is maintain aircraft control. Army chopper pilots always impressed me with their professionalism. Among them, Dustoffs were our heroes.[10]

THE BIRD WE LOST

Octorber 3, 1968, was a day off, and I was catching up on a multitude of tasks. I walked in the heat over to the base library, a small portable building, hoping there was a seat. Postage-stamp sized, the air-conditioned library was in great demand. Its tan padded seats in a metal frame sagged from constant use. No seats this time. I walked back, caught some sun in the banana lounger while studying the Caribou Dash One flight manual. Though it was not the only publication we needed to know, it sharpened my knowledge of the airplane. It equipped me to more confidently answer the prying flight examiner.

"One of our birds is missing," said one of our guys as he passed me.

"Missing? What do you mean it's missing? Where is it?" *Maybe they've just lost count of the sixteen aircraft assigned to us.*

"We've lost contact with it," he answered. "Operations and the command post are trying to find out where it is or what happened."

We waited hours for more news then the grim account came in. One of our veteran crews was climbing out of Camp Evans on a high downwind. A "hook," a Chinook twin rotor chopper, had departed

LZ Nancy a few minutes before and was descending in a high angle of approach, coming in to land. Their flight paths crossed, and they didn't see each other. The chopper came in high from the Caribou's left, and the faster Caribou came from the Chinook's lower right. The Caribou had the limited cockpit visibility typical of transport aircraft.

One of the rotors passed through the cockpit of the Caribou. Both crews and passengers never had a chance. Our Caribou crashed upside down in a marsh near Camp Evans. The loss devastated us. We had rubbed shoulders with these guys every day.

When Beverly, continuing her undergraduate work at Texas Tech, heard of the accident, she knew from the details of the area, aircraft, and type of mission that I might have been on it. She prayed I wasn't.

The squadron asked me to conclude affairs for one of the crew members. They assigned me the flight mechanic on the Caribou. Sadly, I gathered his personal effects and mailed them to his family. We had a service at the base chapel, where many of us, as a group sang, "Sweet Hour of Prayer."

Forty Caribou crewmen died between 1966 and 1972. They gave their tomorrows so that we might have today and tomorrow.[11]

Bunker Deli

When you touched down at the approach end of the runway, landing to the west, the rest of the strip disappeared from sight. That was the effect of the dipsy-doodle of the Dak Seang runway. After a slight rise, the runway dropped off in elevation. If you didn't touch down at the top, you floated forever until it leveled out at the bottom. As one of our shorter strips, 1,400 feet, you wanted to use the whole runway.

The flip side was landing to the east. Once you touched down, you had 1,000 feet of uphill to come to a stop.

The North Vietnamese Army (NVA) targeted Dak Seang, an isolated, critical strip, for ground attacks. Special Forces assisted Montagnard tribesmen to defend their territory.

On one mission, I was a copilot for one of our lieutenant colonels. He failed to touch down at the top, floated all the way to the bottom, and scraped off the tread on a couple of tires with strong braking. One tire was left hanging on the rim, and another tire departed the aircraft. We taxied gingerly back uphill to the ramp on the two inflated tires. It would take a UH-1H Huey a half day to come with tires.

As we waited, I took 8mm movies of the fascinating, smiling array of villagers in the area of the runway, the families of the indigenous troops. The ladies loved bright colors like red.

A lanky guy with a green beret strode across the runway. "Hi, I'm Don, part of the Special Forces detachment. Sorry about your bird. You guys do a great job. While you are waiting, would you like to see Dak Seang and catch some lunch?"

"Nothing sounds better," we answered.

We walked across the runway into a grizzly, inhospitable hilltop honeycombed with bunkers, barbed wire, and machine guns. Their complex and their determination awed me.

Don explained, "Though the Army first came here in 1964, we came into the picture in 1966. The Montagnards or 'Yards,' are an incredible people, defending their own villages against the NVA."

He took us to the command bunker two stories below ground. When necessary, the Green Berets would even call down airstrikes on their own position when overrun and driven underground. They shared their lunch with us, beefy Stateside-style sandwiches instead of C rations.

We left with a deep respect for the work of the Special Forces and the Montagnards, a French word meaning "mountain people."

A few days later, I airdropped my thank you: crates of chickens to my friends the Yards. When the crates hit the runway, they broke open. The small, agile tribesmen chased chickens all around the runway. I saw lost cargo; they saw chicken dinner.[12]

What Was That?

The explosion of gray smoke and flame a couple of miles in front of us, at our altitude, jarred us. Nothing clued us to the reason. "What was that?" we said to each other.

On July 23, 1968, we were flying feet-wet off the coast of Hue and had not yet come to our ten-click turn to head inland to Camp Evans. Way out in front of our aircraft, at our level, I saw an explosion, and out of the explosion, an F-4 descending and turning inland. Its crash into the beach at full speed shocked us.

Wow! I hope nobody was in it.

As we approached the place where I had seen the explosion, we saw a Jolly Green rescue chopper over the water picking up a downed flyer. We did not know what we had seen until reading *Stars and Stripes* a few days later.

When we pieced the facts together, we discovered that the pilot of the F-4 was Major General Robert F. Worley, vice commander of Seventh Air Force. His bird was an RF-4C reconnaissance aircraft with cameras. As Strobe Zero-One, he had taken ground fire flying low-level reconnaissance sixty-five miles northwest of Da Nang. After receiving battle damage in the front of the aircraft, he had flown out to the coast, back toward Da Nang. Fliers have a better chance for rescue bailing out over water.

Worley evidently felt damage to his aircraft or the urgency of his or his back-seater's wounds, precluded landing. Away from a strip like Da Nang, there was also no runway of the length needed by an F-4. He told the guy in back (GIB) to eject, which caused the explosion we saw.

Why did Worley not eject also? Was he too badly wounded? Had the vacuum from the GIB's ejection drawn fire or smoke into his cockpit? The questions remain unanswered today.

Tragically, he died in the F-4 that impacted the beach.

He had a distinguished military career. When Pearl Harbor occurred, he was already a P-40 pilot in the Army Air Corps, and his first command was the 314th Fighter Squadron. On one mission, shot down by the Luftwaffe, he bellied in his aircraft, evaded capture, and returned on foot. He concluded his combat tour commanding P-47N Thunderbolts and finished with 120 aerial missions and the Silver Star. I honor his memory.

Accounts of his distinguished military career can be found on the Internet.[13] He was the highest-ranking US Air Force officer to die in the Vietnam conflict.[14]

Commander's Call

"Commander's Call tonight at 1900 hours. Everybody there, especially you new guys. No excuses." The ops officers repeated the call down the halls several times during morning launch. Notices placarded operations, the lounge, and barracks. Because daily flying moved fast, we newly arrived pilots needed the bigger picture.

The meeting happened on the squadron's second floor. Though uniforms were not required, I was surprised to see some arriving in T-shirts and flip flops. There must have been forty-five or fifty of us.

"Welcome, gentlemen, especially the new guys," Colonel Wolfe, our commander, began. "We'll try to keep this short. Among us is a wide variety of experience. Some of you finishing your tours lived in tents at An Khe. You new guys, gather all the information you can from the old heads."

We second lieutenants clammed up and listened.

"We are all busy but keep up on the classified intelligence at the ops desk. Don't make us chase you around to get it signed off."

Our Executive Commander chimed in.

"You new pilots have a mountain of information to climb. When not flying, stay glued to your Dash One and the operations manual. Save the suntan for later, closer to your R & R.

"I hope I only need to mention once that any guy crawling out under the wire to reach the girls in town is playing with fire." One of our veteran pilots had habitually ignored the warning.

"Don't fly low level. Small arms fire reaches 3,000 feet. Charlie's bullet may have your name on it.

"Most of us enjoy liquid refreshment when relaxing. Remember? 'Eight hours from bottle to throttle.' And our rule is even stiffer. Alcohol-free eight hours before wake-up.

"Though half our missions are dedicated to the Cav, a change may be in the works. Look for a shift toward the special forces camps in the highlands.

"Talking about the Cav, approach the dense helicopter traffic at Camp Evans with extreme caution. We have heard that some of the old heads turn their radios off."

Next up was stan-eval (standardization and evaluation) who trained and flight-checked everybody who flew. Their tongues were always hanging out with exhaustion. "Always use your checklist in every phase of flying. Guys that land gear up make all of us look bad." They reminded us.

"The Caribou is fabulous to learn flying. You new guys think you already know everything. But upgrading to Aircraft Commander, when you make all the decisions, will shift your flying into high gear."

Our commanders finished with some embarrassing details applied to men living in close proximity such as cleanliness in the bathrooms and showers.

Finally, Colonel Richardson offered: "BBQ at my hooch Saturday night. I'm cooking."

We soaked up the information to survive the year.

Bangkok

"**D**rury. Pack your bags. Next Monday you go to Bangkok."

The news lit up my routine existence.

Once or twice during the year all the pilots rotated to Bangkok, Thailand. Two Caribous were rotated there to support the US effort in Thailand. The Don Muang Airbase shared runways with Bangkok airport, jammed with air traffic. The cargo-carrying missions were simple, short, and interesting. They left time to see the city. The country's buildings, especially temples, showed stunning beauty and color, portions covered with gold.

The flight to Bangkok was slow but scenic, including views of tropical islands. We were on vacation. Somebody else back at our home base suffered with the heavy lifting.

"Jon, we don't fly for a couple of days. Do you want to do the Floating Market tour?" one of the veteran pilots asked.

The delights of Bangkok exploded around us. The Floating Market tour joined the Thai people in a shopping delight of sights, sounds, and senses. The small boats travelled canals densely lined with homes and vendors. Beautiful fruit, oranges, papayas, and mangos mixed with vegetables such as cabbages and beans, were all being hawked by enthusiastic vendors.

The European cultural influence surprised me, as I was accustomed to US culture and food. One of my favorites was French onion soup at the Carlton Hotel. Though still serving our tour in a war zone, we stayed in the Chaophya Hotel like tourists and dined in restaurants like civilians. We had shoes custom-made in a day or two by good craftsmen, and many had suits tailored. Some shopped for jewelry and precious stones available at a fraction of the cost elsewhere.

Despite the city's delights, rampant prostitution seemed to be a sad feature. One of the pilots in the mission to Bangkok chose a girl to live with while there and said, "What my wife doesn't know won't hurt her." I questioned his choice as I had seen the premise fail for one of my friends, a World War II flyer. When his wife learned of his unfaithfulness, he justified himself with, "She should never have found out." Their marriage never recovered.

To my surprise, I later learned that in many parts of the world a portion of the sex trade is slavery. The immorality offered by the city went far beyond prostitution; even children were offered.

On one occasion near my hotel, a dolled-up girl with a cab beckoned me saying, "You come wis me." She would have to find customers elsewhere.

But the opportunity was present in Vietnam also. It was said that one of our guys had even hired one of the hootch maids who cleaned our barracks.

THE PLUSES

An Khe, the normal first stop of the day during the first half of my year, had its pluses and minuses. The smell of human waste and the urination tubes in back of the ALCE gagged you. A minus, to be sure.

The base had been carved out to support the mission of the Cav and had originally been called the Golf Course because of idealistic plans to clear all the brush. It was also called Camp Radcliffe, honoring a gunship pilot lost early in the Cav's mission. Tremendously busy, the base had a good ALCE that knew what was happening with each bird's mission for that day.

We still had some of the pilots who had flown from there during its tent era before Phu Cat was completed.

At times, when needed, I would refuel my own aircraft. The task was dangerous. It meant climbing on the roof of my plane and walking out on the wing. I was then passed the heavy nozzle and hose from the truck and filled the tanks from the top of the wings.

But then An Khe had its pluses.

One morning on our way in, my IP Aubray said, "Did you hear that guy on ALCE's freq [frequency] say that the Donut Dollies are at An Khe?"

"The who? What does that mean?"

"The Red Cross brings American girls, volunteers, to serve donuts and coffee to the troops at various locations as a morale builder."

All the way from the An Khe pass, I strained my eyes to see if the Donut Dollies were beside the ramp. On final approach, I could see the tables and wagons with red crosses were there. Long lines of soldiers waited at each coffee and donut station. The Donut Dollies generated huge interest. By this time, most guys had not seen a pretty American female, a round-eye, for weeks or months. My heart nearly jumped out of my flight suit. They reminded of my own dolly, my brown-eyed Beverly, back home.

Normally I respected my brothers in the Army but, *Dang. Why do there have to be so many of them in line?* Even though we had limited turnaround time, we had to wait in line with everyone else.

I treasured my donut and coffee from the angelic Dolly.

After having our senses stunned, Aubray and I lifted off from An Khe and again crossed the Bong Son river on a pristine day.

Though An Khe had its negatives, today the stop had been worth it.

Heaven in Hawaii

The year in Vietnam dragged on forever. It seemed as if I had never had another life and never would. The mind-numbing agony, separated from my wife and a normal existence, droned on day after day.

The great light in my consciousness was the possibility of R & R, allowed once in our one-year tour. I and others debated endlessly the most desirable of the nine locations. Though the nearer sites allowed five days of R & R, because Australia and Hawaii took extra travel time, they were seven days, and they were popular. Beverly and I chose Hawaii, just before Christmas, 1968. Honolulu and Waikiki Beach would be our oyster.

I took a flight to DaNang to take the "freedom bird," the moniker for both the flight to R & R and the final flight to home. Before departing, I changed my funny money to US dollars.

In the back of the stretched DC-8, I visited with an Army guy. "Where do you serve?" I asked.

"I'm in tanks."

"What's going on there?"

"Almost my whole company was wiped out in an NVA ambush. Not many of us left."

His statement delivered a sucker punch to my gut.

In Honolulu, we received the traditional lei, but the real welcome would have to wait. We all sat for two hours of lecture on the moral dangers of R & R. Every minute I agonized, *Get me out of here.*

Beverly and I had reserved an apartment at Fort DeRussy, the former Shore Battery Randolph of World War II. Back then, its fourteen-inch guns fired only once, in practice, shattering windows at the Royal Hawaiian Hotel.

Being together was heaven. We loved the beach, tourist areas, shopping, and restaurants. Though we wrote regularly when separated, there was a world to tell. We were able to catch up on our lives, Beverly's schooling at Texas Tech, and our friends in Lubbock. After my departure for Vietnam, things had changed for her. She dropped into a new world where she was neither a single nor a couple. She didn't fit anywhere.

Bill, a lieutenant from administration at Phu Cat, came on R & R at the same time. We did many things together with him and his wife. With our new freedom, we were full of antics and took 8mm movies of our stunts. The girls posed for model shots by the shore. At the zoo, behind some bars, we pretended to be wild animals. I did a stunt with a garbage can where I seemed to come up out of the can after a night's sleep.

Five days flashed by then came another good-bye. Our consolation—in five months we would be together again.

Santa Bou

How do you re-engage in the Vietnam War after the heaven of R & R?

The transition came quick. Colonel Richardson snagged me in the hall when I returned.

"Have a minute, Drury?"

"Sure, Colonel, what's up?"

"You and I are flying the Santa Bou on Christmas day."

"Last year, the 483rd decorated one of the Bous with Santa's face and called it a Santa Bou. They took Christmas cheer and gifts to Special Forces camps in isolated strips. The idea was so well received that this year all six squadrons will fly a Santa Bou. Ours is Christmas day."

I am not sure why I was chosen; perhaps because I served in civic action.

"Where do we get the things to deliver to the troops?" I asked.

"That's our challenge. Our gifts will come from our own guys in the 537th. They'll have a chance to contribute food, beverages, candy, and toys."

Our aircraft was painted like Santa's face. The radome was painted red like Rudolph's nose. Blue eyes with white eyebrows were painted above, and a bushy white beard was painted below.

The birds of other units were painted variously, some just saying Merry Christmas and Happy New Year.

Major networks provided press coverage.

We enjoyed the role of bringing good things to the Army and Special Forces troops we served. Maybe our good food and Christmas cheer would be a touch of home for those who had the hardest slugging of Vietnam, the infantry.

We flew into camps we had come to serve in the last half of the year, delivering candy, presents, gifts, goodies, and Christmas dinner.

One squadron decorated the inside of the Santa Bou with a fireplace, complete with Christmas trimmings. In another, a flight engineer dressed up as Santa handing gifts to Special Forces personnel.

Our 483rd Commander, Colonel Christensen, commended our effort.

Army commander Col. Donald M. Wood noted hours invested in the creative decoration of the planes, adding, "We appreciate all the thoughtfulness your unit expressed to make this Christmas a most enjoyable and memorable one."

General Creighton Abrams, overall commander in Vietnam, noted ". . . your project 'Santa Bou' during the Christmas season has earned both the respect and gratitude of Americans and Vietnamese alike."

Nice to start the final part of my tour with serving the troops.[15]

A Journey of Faith

Don't *get close to anybody. You never know who will stick you!*
My loner rubric constructed in childhood to avoid pain still shielded me in later college years. I wore my dad's brown World War II Army jacket to protect me from unwanted human contact. The high point of my existence was packing my 30.06 on my motorcycle and swooping down draws to a large firing range in the woods. My solitary journey did not provide satisfying answers for life, and at the end of college, I considered faith, something I had avoided up to then.

As I considered a new framework for living, John, a Christian worker, challenged me to engage ten study books on Bible topics. The summary of Bible truths he introduced proved deeply satisfying. I had to add the new study to university coursework. Because of this new priority, I started each morning in a library study carrel.

More foreign was the invitation to engage in learning with a group of other college students. Though a new way of life, studying the Bible with others also proved satisfying.

On arrival at Phu Cat, I found men of faith at the base chapel. I met men like Ken, a sergeant and a quiet, sincere believer, and Dave, also a sergeant and a lay preacher. In my shallow faith, I also encountered things I did not understand. Dave, though of fervent faith, did not participate in communion, a church ordinance remembering Christ's death. It was because his church back in the States practiced what they called, "closed communion."

Frustrating also was the experience with another chaplain, who held a different framework of faith than mine. Puzzled, I asked, "What motivated you to enter ministry?"

"I like people, and it seemed a good idea," he answered.

Slowly I learned to allow broader parameters for those who embraced faith.

One time, I shared a worry or concern with Dave, my new friend. He answered, "God is still on His throne." Good answer, Dave. I have remembered your answer often.

Foremost among those with whom I engaged was Russ Deal. We would meet during the week to pray and memorize parts of the Bible. He had been nurtured by the Navigators, a Christian ministry active in the US military, centered on Bible study and values of strong character. He felt he had not lived up to their standards. One leader told him that if he did not submit to the instructions given him, he wouldn't make it. I disagreed as Russ was one of the finest men I knew.

Though comradeship in values of faith was new, contact with men such as these deepened my spiritual growth.

Ready for the NVA

D on wore baggy green air police fatigues, a big smile, and sergeant stripes. I am not sure where I met him. As part of the canine squad, he patrolled the perimeter with his black and white German shepherd.

"Don, you guys must practice with your handguns and M-16s on a range. Where is it, and would they let anybody practice there?"

"Are you fixing to plug some poor hapless NVA on one of your missions?"

"I'm more of a danger to myself than the NVA," I answered. "They issue a .38 Smith and Wesson when I go out on missions, and I would like to practice."

"It's not much of a range, mostly a collection of discards and burned garbage in an open area on the south edge of the base. Sure, I think anybody could practice there." He described how to reach the range.

Shooting brought back great memories of college. I remembered riding my motorcycle on Saturdays, my US surplus .30-06 Garand strapped to the side of the bike, heading to a firing range. The ten-mile trip traversed rolling hills outside Oakland, California.

The large marksmanship site had more than six ranges. Later I would take boys there to learn to safely shoot .22 rifles.

Though I could not afford expensive equipment, I had begun to reload my own shells and found the accuracy better than ammunition off the shelf.

My father had purchased a couple of rifles through the National Rifle Association: an 8mm German Mauser and a World War II M-1 Carbine. I loved handling and shooting all of them.

At my unit, my next stop was the armorer. "When I have a day off, may I check out my .38 and go practice at the air police shooting range?"

"Sure, no problem. Just sign it out and bring it back when you are through."

"Do I pay for the ammo?" I queried.

"Nope, It's all part of the war."

Are you kidding me? Free ammunition. In the States ammo can cost an arm and a leg.

"Do I need to clean it before I bring it back?"

"No, I'll take care of that."

When the time came, I figured thirty rounds was enough for my practice. When I was a duty officer and not needed elsewhere, I took the squadron six-pax truck and looped around the base perimeter to the ramshackle range.

This must be it, I decided. Having no paper targets, I shot some metal drums already plugged full of holes.

The times I went, I never found anyone else there. I could shoot to my heart's content. And if Charlie came around the corner, I was ready for him.

MARS

"Beverly, this is Jon. I am calling from MARS. How are you? Over."

A station on the red planet?

MARS (Military Auxiliary Radio System) enabled a shortwave radio link between service personnel overseas and their families back in the States.

In the day of cell phones and Skype, it is hard to realize the big role shortwave radio played during the Vietnam War. During World War II, radio amateurs were denied access to the airwaves. Following the war, the US Army reactivated the former Auxiliary Amateur Radio System (AARS). Civilian radio operators were then trained and licensed, and the radio network was renamed MARS.

Longing for a miraculous phone connection to home, we went to MARS on a day off and waited our turn, whether general or buck private. The plain gray building lay in a remote part of the base. Inside it looked like soldiers lived there. The long worn-out couches and chairs, thrashed magazines and papers, said thousands of GIs had waited and slept here.

When you arrived, few or many troops might be waiting in line to place a call. Some guys were desperate to get their calls out. Many had received heartbreaking "Dear John" letters, dumped by their girl or wife back in the States. They were the most desperate, trying to mend the tie. Others were trying to gather information about a newborn son or daughter.

When shortwave receptivity, called "propagation," was poor, we waited endlessly and often returned to our barracks disappointed.

When someone shouted, "They're getting through!" all the green forms draped around the room jerked to instant alertness. Then, the line might move quickly, because calls were not allowed to be lengthy.

"Drury," the operator hollered from his radio booth. Entering the booth, I was told to sit in a gray and brown government-issued chair right next to the operator and his set. The sound-proofed booth eliminated outside sounds, including jet fighter takeoffs. You and the person you were talking to had to say, "Over," each time you finished a line of communication.

Having connected to a stateside radio operator willing to place my call to Beverly, I usually reached her in the middle of the night.

"Beverly, this is Jon. I'm calling from the MARS station. How are you? Over."

Beverly, in no sense awake, answered, "It's the middle of the night." *What is it the Air Force does not understand about the middle of the night,* she was asking.

"Ma'am, please say, 'Over.'"

Beverly answers, "Over."

I question, "How is school going?"

"Sir, please remember to say, 'Over.'"

"Over," I obediently added.

Beverly answered, "Fine."

"Ma'am, please remember to say 'Over.'"

Club Phu Cat

The line inched forward at the Officer's Club as I waited to order my steak and baked potato on an evening. *Why can't we order from a waitress like normal people do*, I fumed. We not only waited to order, but service took forever, and the Club was jammed by those ready to relax.

Because most of us had no capability to cook for ourselves, we had to depend on the chow hall or the Officer's Club for meals. Colonel Richardson, our Executive Commander, had a grill where he would periodically grill meals for one or all. The rest of us had fewer choices.

The O Club at Phu Cat offered a respite from routine chow hall faire. Though small and plain compared to its stateside equivalent, it was close to our barracks until we relocated to more distant digs. Overly air conditioned, it offered a welcome change from tropical heat we had toiled through during the day.

Lunch was an easier time to hit the Club. Those not flying could grab a hamburger with coke or other liquid refreshment. The service was never fast, but it happened.

The Vietnamese waitresses in the club raised the suspicion we were encouraged to cultivate. "Are they secretly Viet Cong cadre members? Suspect everybody!" I never saw anything but faithful service from the Vietnamese who served us. One waitress, especially beautiful, was said to be married to a Special Forces officer. Another large waitress boasted that she weighed 100 kilo, or 220 pounds.

For some reason, all ordered and waited in line at an inordinately small window. Perhaps they wanted all orders to go through one channel because money changed hands. We paid for everything in MPC (military payment currency), green money being illegal.

Time to jump ship, I concluded. Because I was not waiting for anyone to eat with me, I left the line and walked the warm but peaceful 150 feet to the chow hall. From the overcooked fried chicken, I picked out the more edible pieces, leaving the crusty and greasy portions.

Because the club was so jammed at night, I normally chose the quieter course of eating in the chow hall. It also left more time for the books, and with the busyness of the flying schedule, I was scratching for every moment I could find to study. It was satisfying to finally take ground on studying the airplane and procedures in-country. *I'm actually learning this stuff.*

Course Correction

"Jon, why are you so religious?"

The question, asked by John, a fellow pilot, came one noon in September 1968. Five of us copilots, in cutoffs and flip-flops, were finishing our lunch in the Club. Asked at a lull in the conversation, the query caught me flat-footed. No one had ever asked that question.

"I haven't always been interested in issues of faith," I answered, trying to give some background. "In junior college, I ran around with the party crowd, trying to find happiness and fulfillment. They seemed to have found it.

"Concerning faith, I reasoned: I have only one life. Why be religious and miserable? I think faith in God must mean wearing missionary clothes, carrying a black Bible, and suffering from endless boredom. In my false conception, I was pretty sure that was what God wanted. I saw people of faith as demented, wild-eyed fanatics, pouncing on the unconvinced."

A couple guys in the group smiled. It seemed they could identify.

"Through four years, my pursuit for elusive happiness deflated like an empty hot air balloon. I didn't know what I believed, but I was troubled also because my university proclaimed that everything was relative. There were no absolutes or concrete values, no rights or wrongs.

"My only concession to God was that at the end of college, He and I would have a final talk, a little set-to. Then I would go my own way. I had planned out my life, and God was not part of the picture.

"My final talk with God came unhinged. At a college retreat, I saw my search for fulfillment had crashed and burned. On my own, I did not have any satisfying answers for life. On a test basis, I turned back to God, Jesus Christ, and the Bible."

A couple of the guys looked puzzled. My choices represented a different universe for them.

"Back at school for my final quarter, I began reading a Bible from the university book store, seeking what God wanted me to do next. I studied Bible truths in a set of study books along with other students. A sense of peace began to grow.

"This new course began to fill my life. I now see flying the Bou as part of this new way of life that I might call serving God."

"Interesting," John replied. "Not my path, but interesting."

Later one of the guys who listened told me he did not accept my conclusions. I respected his response.

Another fellow flyer declared, "I know God, but I choose not to follow Him right now."

A third pilot, not in on the Club discussion, said, "I see what you believe and want it for myself."

NVA Prisoner of War

"When you were working up there in the left corner of the aircraft, you had your back turned on that NVA. He could have gone for your gun!"

"What?" I shot back to the man who said it.

"That NVA up front could have gone for your gun!"

Plugged by the North Vietnamese in my own airplane? The thought shocked me to my core. What would have happened if he had pulled my weapon? There was no strap on it. He just had to draw the .38 S & W out of its holster on my hip.

I was assisting on a flight where I was not one of the pilots. The Caribou was jammed, every seat filled. We were transporting an NVA sergeant who was headed to a POW (Prisoner of War) camp with his escort. We were flying in the highlands in the western part of Vietnam. In order to keep an eye on the man and to prevent any tricks, we placed him in the most forward seat on the right.

Enemy combatants were encouraged to defect and join the South Vietnamese forces. Enemy troop locations received air drops of Chieu

183

Hoi (Open Arms) leaflets, offering the opportunity to surrender.[26] Some who changed sides became scouts for the South.

After their capture, prisoners were normally turned over to the South Vietnamese, who ran the POW camps. The largest camp was at An Thoi on Phu Quoc Island. At one point, it held 35,000 Viet Cong and NVA prisoners. One Army pilot who transported many enemy prisoners said they always had a bag placed over their heads by the South Vietnamese. He felt they would have received more compassionate treatment from Americans. True, our prisoner had no bag over his head, though he wore his North Vietnamese uniform.

During the flight, I assisted the crew with items in the front of the cargo compartment. We stored things there that we did not immediately need for flight like manuals and forms. Because I wasn't up in the cockpit on the flight, I wore my issued handgun. We carried the pistols on every flight, but we stowed them out of way when in the cockpit. Wearing the weapon hindered our climbing in and out of the cockpit.

What might have happened if he had snatched my .38? Would he have tried to commandeer the airplane? Would the fifteen armed soldiers on board have engaged him in a gun battle right in the cargo compartment?

Thankfully, I will never know.

AirStrikes

In places, the landscape in South Vietnam looked like Swiss cheese due to airstrikes. Bomb craters that had filled with water could be red, blue, or any color. It was fascinating to watch airstrikes in progress. You wondered about the conflict on the ground that spawned the strikes.

Directed by forward air controllers (FACs), these pilots coordinated air-ground operations, which meant close air support for ground troops. They usually flew highly maneuverable O-1 or O-2 high-wing airplanes in which their vision below would be less restricted. They might direct single fighter-bombers making a strike, but sometimes multiple fighters took their turns rolling in on the target. A FAC might pinpoint the target with smoke then say, "Fastmover One-Two, hit 50 feet west of my smoke."

I respected the difficult work of the FACs. My friend Lew served as a FAC in the Korean War. He flew an Aeronca L-16 there, a taildragger I later enjoyed flying out of Livermore, California. Lew went on to fly A-1Es in Vietnam.

The big bomb strikes were B-52 Arc Light missions, typically in areas of concentrated enemy activity such as the Ho Chi Minh trail. The B-52 was called the "most terrifying weapon of the war." Originally designed to carry nuclear weapons, it was modified to carry 500- to1,000- pound iron bombs. With a bomb capacity of 60,000 pounds, it had ten times the capacity of the World War II B-17. Usually flying in a formation of three aircraft, coming from Anderson Airbase in Guam, they flew grueling nine-hour missions.

In theory, print intelligence and broadcast warnings prepared you for the hazard. Sometimes we were warned on GUARD channel, heard by all airborne traffic prior to the strike. But I doubt the warning was made in every case. If you heard it, it was best to listen. I estimate we knew about the strikes about one-third of the time.

The force of the strikes amazed us. They often carpet-bombed enemy basecamps in forests and mountains. Often, we were too distant to see individual bombs falling, but nobody could miss the huge track of explosions in the forest.

But the unthinkable did happen—your worst nightmare. Some guys ended up in the middle of Arc Light strikes, bombs falling all around them, though I never heard of an aircraft hit and downed because of the strikes.

Aircraft Commander

AIRCRAFT COMMANDER

"I have approval to begin your upgrade to Aircraft Commander. How does that sound?"

The statement came from Aubray Abrams, my instructor pilot, on a mission we flew in February 1969.

"That sounds fabulous. How many rides will it take?" I asked.

As a copilot, I sat in the right seat of the cockpit. I faced a steep learning curve. The aircraft commander (A/C) in the left seat made all the crucial decisions. An instructor could put me in either seat as part of instruction. Upgrade to First Pilot let me fly from either seat, but still the Aircraft Commander made all the decisions.

Being an A/C was the top of the food chain.

I checked out as a copilot for the 537th in June 1968, and as First Pilot in November. Since my knowledge and experience had grown, the transitions felt natural and comfortable.

To my question about the number of missions, Aubray answered, "Three or four. We will do everything you might be asked to do on a mission and beyond."

The upgrade became twenty-five short field landings on three missions, fifteen short field takeoffs, about eight flying hours per mission. Though all was done under the microscope of an instructor pilot, my confidence grew.

After the training flights, Aubray said, "We did it. We got everything done. You'll get a flight check in a couple of days." I passed the upgrade check three days later with Maj. Dan Yost.

Soon after, having not yet flown my first A/C mission, a call came for a load to Plei Me, our most difficult strip at 1,100 feet. At Ops, two duty officers debated.

"Two days! That's all the time Drury has been a qualified A/C. He's never flown an A/C mission."

"He's got the wings. Let's let him fly it," the other answered.

Matched with a copilot, we picked up our load at Pleiku then flew to Plei Me, forty-four kilometers to the west. I could see the triangular outline of the Special Forces camp as I set up to land from the west. During October and November 1965, the NVA attacked the base, but reinforcements drove them back.

A good touchdown and reversed props raised the cloud of dust normal for a Bou on a dirt strip—zero-zero visibility for a few seconds. We shut down at the wide dirt space at the end of the strip. It was all they had for ramp space. The mass of shell casings and expended brass caught my eye. Someone had fought the bad guys here.

I did not return to Plei Me often, but my first A/C trip there left a feeling of accomplishment.[16]

Bailout Rescue

Sometimes I hear comments about rivalry among the military services, but as a Caribou pilot flying short-field combat missions in Vietnam, my experience was the opposite. Two stories come to mind.

I helped launch our eight birds one morning. Afterward, I grabbed one of the precious sodas from the fridge in the lounge and caught my breath. I glanced at the mounted, captured AK-47 wondering *What stories would that gun tell if it could talk?* The operations officer had nothing else for me, so I took the six-pax truck to the base exchange then caught a quick after-launch nap in the barracks.

A rap on my door ended my mid-morning reverie. They needed me down at operations. Maintenance needed an engine test on a Bou in a revetment facing the runway.

I loved starting the R2000 Pratt and Whitney engines, and this mill ran smoothly, the sweet music of hammers on a tin sheet.

While running the engine and logging the results, I monitored tower frequency and was surprised to hear my friend Rick, an F-100 pilot, calling tower with a flight emergency. He was coming back to Phu

Cat with damage to his engine. An F-100 has only one engine. If that quits, it gets quiet. I would learn the concept over Cheo Reo. All pilots are trained to make a dead-stick landing without power, but a modern fighter has the aerodynamics of an anvil. It is a risky, dangerous business and is not recommended. Below a certain altitude not even an ejection seat can save you.

Rick turned a high downwind at about 2,000 feet then realized his engine had gone too far south for a safe landing.

"I'm going," he said on tower frequency and ejected. The jet ejection system rocketed him above the airplane. Then I saw his chute billow. The pilotless aircraft impacted a range of hills to the south, an explosion of fire and smoke.

I saw that Rick's parachute descent would take him into rice paddies, far outside the base perimeter. The bad guys owned that turf. I punched the mike button.

"Tower, the F-100 punched out on downwind. You better get that rescue helicopter churning." We had one or two rescue helicopters dedicated to Phu Cat.

Rick told me the rest of the story in person. "I no sooner hit the rice paddy than a guy's hands grabbed the front of my flight suit and threw me bodily inside something."

It wasn't the bad guys. It was an Army Dustoff medevac Huey helicopter. On any given day, these guys were spring-loaded to give their lives for us.

Our turn to reciprocate would come at Duc Lap II.

Competition or Comradeship?

uc Lap II was an undulating rubberized strip, two miles from Cambodia. A boxy French tank rusted beside the runway, remainder of a French defeat in the 1950s. A few months before we got there, Special Forces and Vietnamese units repelled a determined NVA attack. The deep green of wooded ridges bordered the strip on the north and west. Rolls of concertina barbed wire and dirty walls of sand bags outlined bunker positions.

We arrived at the 2,300-foot strip on our last mission for the day, and what we found was anything but a routine load. An Army sergeant in sweat-stained fatigues walked out to meet us.

"Our whole unit is clearing out of these two hills. We're the last to go. Our twenty troops go and so does our radio equipment piled up over there."

After our crew looked at their pile of radio equipment, we knew we had a problem.

"Sergeant, taking this whole load of men and equipment exceeds our gross weight limitations. We can take half the load today, and other transports can come back tomorrow. This is our last mission of the day. It is your decision what goes first: men, equipment, or half and half."

Worried, the sergeant answered "If you leave any of these men here, you will probably carry them out in body bags. There's an NVA trail right over there." He pointed north of the hills and the strip. "And we can't go without our equipment."

Every airplane is made to withstand a greater load than listed in the published limits. They don't tell you how much more. We loaded the radio gear around the center of gravity, marked by a red line, and strapped the troops in front and in back of the load. We taxied to the very end of the strip, ran the engines up to full power, came off the brakes, and started our roll. The strip had some dips, and we rolled through each one. A Caribou normally takes off in 600 feet, but we probably used 1,200 feet of the strip to gain airspeed, then pulled it off very gently, thinking about wing root attaching points. As we made a turn to the north, we pilots looked at each other and smiled. Simultaneously we both said, "If we had lost an engine, we probably would have bought the farm."

Our flight to Ban Me Thuot, a provincial capital, a dust bowl of airplanes, temporary buildings, and troops, was not long.

It was our turn to risk ourselves for them. In combat, comradeship, not competition, more defines how the service branches relate to each other.

SILENCE OVER CHEO REO

We took off from An Khe on a sunny day in spring 1969, on one of my new missions as an aircraft commander. We took off to the north on runway 03 then turned crosswind to climb around Hon Con or Monkey Mountain, scarred by aircraft crashes because it rose so abruptly from the high plain. We headed south, climbed over jungle, then leveled at 4,000 feet, going south over Cheo Reo, a V-shaped airstrip we serviced periodically. Getting to altitude was always one of the nicest parts of the flight after the heavy work of loading cargo in the tropical heat. But cruise sometimes generated brainless euphoria.

Whoosh! All of a sudden, both engines quit. We hit a wall of air, decelerating quickly with neither engine pulling. "What in the fat!" My copilot and I both jerked into action, reaching for controls, trying to solve a double engine failure. Looking at my copilot, I realized that he had pulled back both mixtures to "shutoff," which is exactly what the engines did. At altitude, we always ran the cruise checklist in which we moved the mixture levers overhead to "auto lean" to conserve fuel. My first mistake was doing that checklist silently by myself. My copilot, thinking that we had not done the cruise checklist, also silently, did it himself. Wanting to move the mixture levers, instead of moving them one at a time as the checklist requires, he pulled both back at once to the next stop—shutoff!

All I could think to do was to say, "Put them back in!" He hesitated, so I moved the mixtures back to auto lean myself, and the engines came alive again. At the time, I did not remember that I needed to retard the prop levers to be sure we did not get an overspeed, but we did not, and again we were flying. In my intense relief, I did not berate my copilot. I owned my part of the fault.

We had again proven the old saw: What's flying like? Hours of boredom interspersed by moments of stark terror.[17]

THEY WERE SHOOTING at YOU

"They were shooting at you around base and final," my copilot exhaled as he returned to the cockpit.

"What?" I replied, lurching to alert in my seat. "Who said that?"

"The loader," he replied.

The Army base of Ben Het perched on a bluff, six miles from the tri-border area of Laos, Cambodia, and South Vietnam. Created in 1968, it challenged the infiltration route the NVA favored to move troops and supplies from the Ho Chi Minh trail to the highlands.

Something was always happening there, and one time I saw an NVA armored vehicle on the perimeter of the base that had been knocked out in an attack on March 3, 1969.

Every time I landed, there was a new story of enemy fire, including rocket and mortar attacks. The situation changed day by day and hour by hour. Because the base received enemy fire often, we had to make our turnaround as quickly as possible. Often, to avoid fire or mortar rounds, we left the load on the end of the runway, turned around, and departed.

Ready to go as quickly as possible, I remained in the cockpit, and my copilot went back to watch the unloading. When he did, the Army loader said, "They were shooting at you."

When my copilot told me, I answered, "No they weren't!" I had seen no tracers evidencing ground fire. Besides, I was a nice guy. *Why would they shoot at me?* My answer belied my delusion. In normal day-to-day operations, our lumbering, slow bird was not normally targeted. Yet we were resupplying a critical base.

There was a knobby prominence close to our base leg in the traffic pattern when landing from the west. The NVA used it to shoot at transports landing for resupply.

In the intervening years, I came to realize they were indeed shooting at me. The loader knew what he was talking about. He had seen or heard it. At the Caribou Association reunion of September 2011, in Dallas, I met Glenn Ashley of the 5th Special Forces, who served as a medic at Ben Het (A-244) during that period. He experienced a great deal of combat, was wounded multiple times, and was finally evacuated.

I told Glenn about the incident and added, "Of course that was .30 caliber fire, wasn't it?"

He answered, "No, it was probably 12.7mm [the equivalent of .50 caliber]." If the troops could hear the fire, he was probably correct.

Though the North Vietnamese gunner did not hit me, a Caribou is a tin can with very simple construction. With better aim by the gunner he could have made us Swiss cheese.

Ben Het Incoming

Oh great, now what do I do with my load of eight-inch artillery ammunition?

My frustration came on seeing a mushroom explosion and small cloud of smoke erupt in the marsh beside the runway at Ben Het. I was on downwind of the landing pattern. I could not see rounds landing inside the perimeter of the base because I was over it.

My mission had originated on the flight line at our small outpost in Pleiku. There we coordinated loads destined for Special Forces and Army camps in the highlands. Some of those loads were food or live animals, and sometimes we airdropped them. Because the enemy targeted Pleiku with mortar or rocket rounds, we protected our outpost with sandbags.

When I got my load, the major commanding our detachment directed me, "If Ben Het is taking incoming, do not go into the base."

After takeoff, I flew down the road to Ben Het, past Kontum and Dak To II, and when I arrived opposite the runway, I could see a mortar or rocket round land in the marsh south of the runway. The enemy might have been zeroing-in their weapon. Were they targeting the marsh beside the runway to be sure I saw it? Were they saying, "Just try landing; we're saving our best for you."

The situation brought up an interesting question. *How badly does Ben Het need this ammunition?* If they say the need is desperate, then I have to decide whether I am going to go in despite the major's orders.

I could land, dump it at the end of the runway, then take off the opposite direction. I might be able to get in and out without being hit. At times, we had to drop our load that way.

Of course, I might be court-martialed for disobeying the major's orders. There is a small, fine line between a medal and a court-martial.

I radioed the base on FM radio, the frequency we used to coordinate our work with Ben Het, and asked, "I am the Caribou in the pattern, and I am carrying eight-inch artillery ammunition. How badly do you need this stuff?"

The troop on the other end of the radio just hollered, "We're taking incoming. I'm going to the bunker." Repeated calls received no response. He was in the bunker.

I returned to Pleiku with my load. *O well, at least it looked like I was willing to follow orders.*[18]

Lights and Loading at Phu Bai

Late morning, we descended into Hue Phu Bai, picking our way through fleecy cumulus clouds. Airborne, our landing lights were on, always. Yep! There was another bird, a camouflaged C-123 Provider climbing through the same hole we were using. We banked quickly to the right, and he did the same.

A big, forgiving runway and a faded control tower, welcomed us to the Hue Phu Bai airport. The nearby former capital of Hue had been the site of battles during Big Tet, 1968. As headquarters of several large units, Phu Bai was a major port for air cargo.

Jammed with traffic on a congested ramp, we created ramp space that was part grass. It seemed every transport aircraft in Vietnam was here. Louie, a buck private, screeched to a halt in his forklift in a cloud of dust. "Sorry. You're number eight. I can't get here for maybe forty-five minutes." Turning on a dime, he was off.

The field was dusty, deep dusty. In oppressive heat, loading became a tiring, dirty challenge. The forklift drivers worked like slaves—heroes of the operation.

The good news was chow time in the Army aviation mess hall. In contrast to our experience with the Marines at Chu Lai, the Army fliers welcomed us. The mess hall was tent-like in its temporary construction, plain and tick-tacky with an uneven floor laid over dirt. But the barbecued beef sandwiches were amazing, almost Stateside, and the welcome and respect of fellow fliers made everything better. When we needed to stay glued to the aircraft and the loading, we ate boxed C rations, affectionately called "Old sea rats." We carried some on board in case schedule dictated that aged wharf rats were on the menu. But beware of eating C rations regularly, as your weight would balloon. The caloric content was meant for combat soldiers.

When I returned to Stateside flying, I kept the habit of flying with my landing light on, though I was sometimes questioned by flight instructors: "You don't need to do that." They meant it is not required. But it is free visibility, which is worth everything in spotting other birds and their spotting you.

At one strip, the chief mechanic was angered when he saw any of his own planes with a landing light on. From his narrow perspective, the idiot was burning out his precious light bulbs, costing money and parts. On one of my first flights there the operations scheduler came running out when I blocked in, instructing me to never, never land with my landing light on.

But Hue Phu Bai always reminded me of the value of landing lights.

Downed Oscar Deuce

"Beep, beep, beep," a sharp rescue beeper sounded in our headsets on GUARD channel as we flew down the coast. My heart stopped. I did not know what the emergency was. Maybe some fellow aviator had been shot down. Maybe he had bailed out and was in danger or injured. I began praying for him and the rescuers.

Then we got the call. "Soul four-one-six, Qui Nhon ALCE. Since you are in the area, would you mind searching for a downed Oscar Deuce?"

Air rescue happened often in North and South Vietnam. As fliers bailed out from damaged aircraft, particularly in North Vietnam, we would hear the beepers and calls. At times, we could hear rescues in progress. The beeper also sounded in case of a crash landing. In many cases, an HH-53 Jolly Green Giant was involved. The six-bladed helicopter equipped for rescue was able to lower a crewman to assist the injured, sometimes in dense jungle. Often a backup HH-53 flew "high" in case the rescue chopper itself was shot down. Prop-driven A-1E Skyraider "Sandys," assisted in ground fire suppression. If hostile fire was too hot, the rescue had to be terminated. It was an HH-53 that picked up the F-4 GIB in the water at the tragic loss of Colonel Worley.

In many cases, an Army Dustoff Huey performed the pickup as in the case of my F-100 friend, rescued from a rice patty.

"ALCE we'll do everything we can to help. What's up?"

"The O-2 is a FAC missing west of us. It had engine failure, and we think crashed or force-landed."

We thought the O-2 fortunate in having an extra engine. But its pilots said the only benefit of the second engine was enabling you to get to the crash site.

"ALCE, give us an idea where to search."

"He's somewhere in the valleys five clicks west of Qui Nhon."

"We are on our way."

We turned sharply and descended to 1,000 feet, despite the danger of ground fire, for the search. We strained our vision to spot the downed bird. We flew up and down sparsely wooded valleys, often along a river. We searched down low and when we got to the end of a valley, climbed steeply, kicked left or right rudder, and dropped back into the valley to search along another line.

After searching for ten or fifteen minutes, we heard the good news that the pilot had ditched in a river one ridgeline over. He had gotten out of it okay, with no injuries. A huge relief.

Joy flooded me as a brother had been rescued. It could have been me.

Body Run

Wh-en assigned the mission on a Thursday, my skull screamed for relief. *You can't be asking me to do this. How about carrying troops, or ice cream, or artillery ammunition. But not this. Not again.*

Periodically my mission would transit Dong Ha, the northernmost town in Vietnam and the capital of Quang Tri Province. As a strategically important base, it provided surveillance of enemy troop movements across the Demilitarized Zone (DMZ). And Dong Ha held the Marines' graves registration unit

A large, gray Navy refrigeration truck awaited the day's latest arrivals of young Marines. At times, after a big fight, the bodies of those killed in action (KIA) would overflow and line up on the ground outside. Often a Marine chaplain would kneel beside each, pray, and touch the soldier's head or shoulder or attempt to straighten a damaged uniform.

As a temporary graves registration unit, those killed in action were identified, their bodies cared for and prepared for transport to Da Nang and then sent back to the States. Because of the distance from Da Nang, transport was always by air.

That's where we came in. The Caribou could be set up with stanchions that could hold litters, each with a body in a body bag. They would load us with twenty to twenty-four until we had a full load. A full load of bodies

The agony that accompanied the task—each one was somebody's son, somebody's husband, somebody's brother, or somebody's dad. The horror of the losses assaulted me. *How could they be gone? What had gone wrong? What happened to each?* They were questions that screamed for answers, and I had none.

These were young lives, snuffed out in their prime, honored brothers who had given their lives in the cause of freedom. We would lose forty of our own men in the Vietnam mission, three of whom I knew and flew with.

The sickening stench of death was unbearable in the aircraft, and there was only some relief when we could get to altitude. Then open cockpit windows could admit some fresh air. But the stench was more bearable than the horror of these losses.

I did not serve in the US Army or the US Marines, but my feeling was that these were heroes, doing a tougher job than I was doing.

When reviewing these facts, I found a site that gave the pictures of the Marines killed out of Dong Ha. Proud, handsome, some in uniform, some in civvies. I grieved for young lives but could not look at the site for long. I couldn't take it.

Despite my mental anguish, I feel honored to have escorted my brothers in part of their final journey.

WHEN PIGS FLY

"Drury, saddle up. You're taking a couple sows to Dak Pek."

I jumped to action after a morning snooze, laying my head back on the sagging couch. I had flown to Pleiku and parked my bird at the sandbagged command post shack that directed our Pleiku missions.

Animals. Way cool. Something fun, I reflected, although Dak Pek was not my favorite strip because of a hill close to the runway.

The Fifth Special Forces would regularly crate livestock raised by Vietnamese farmers. Cows, pigs, and even chickens were air delivered to their camps. The outposts could butcher the animals or add to herds or pens. Usually, the animals and crates were strapped to a warehouse pallet for ease of loading.

The sows were big. Being crated up and sitting in the heat did not help their temperament.

On one of these missions, the huge, highly irritated sow got out of her crate during flight. When the Flight Mechanic told the pilot that the beast was loose, he said, "Well, try to strap her down or something so we can get to our destination."

The Flight Mech tried his best, but, his own safety in peril, hanging on the steps to the cockpit hollered, "She's mean, and there is no corralling her."

The pilot shouted back, "OK, lower the ramp in flight and let her go before she wrecks the aircraft."

When the ramp began to go down, the pig saw the daylight, and she ran out the back of the aircraft like a shot. Then it was like a cartoon. Suspended in thin air, the pig's startled expression said, "Oh no!" She dropped like an anvil to become someone's pork sandwich.

Often when we could not land at a destination, we would gravity airdrop the cargo by parachute, usually from 200 or 500 feet. Though we could drop a maximum of five pallets, the most in one pass was three because of the need for accuracy.

If the load was not done correctly, it could jam in the cargo compartment once released. The jam might cause the aircraft to lose the critical balance needed for flight. The flight engineer and an additional crew member, a "kicker," insured that the load was released properly.

But for one aircraft, the animals had their revenge. One of the Bous used often for transport of cattle, seemed to get heavier and heavier over the months. It was the feel of the airplane, normally with a maximum gross weight of 28,000 pounds. When the floorboards were removed the mystery was solved—the manure and urine from hundreds of animals had seeped through the floorboards and we had an unexpected load.[19]

DELBERt LOCKWOOD

"An Khe Tower, Soul Four-Oh-Seven has a fire on number one engine. I am returning to the field. Request a straight-in on runway 21."

"Roger, Four-Oh-Seven, understand one burning. The runway is yours. An Khe traffic, hold position for aircraft emergency."

At 300 feet after takeoff, Delbert Lockwood heard an explosion in his left engine. He looked out and saw fire streaming back from the top of the engine. He yanked the throttle back, shut off the fuel, and hit the feather button, streamlining the blades into the wind.

He kept the right engine at maximum power and shot the fire bottle to the left engine while turning right with strong right rudder into a teardrop turn to get back to the runway.

While turning he was shocked to see that the fire bottle had no effect and that the engine was still burning.

After his successful landing, he asked maintenance for the broken R-2000 cylinder which had separated from the engine and blown up into the cowling. He kept the broken jug in a corner of his hootch as a discussion piece.

Clean-cut, professional, and personable, Del Lockwood arrived in the spring of 1969, during the second half of my year at Phu Cat. Of medium height and athletic build, he had a broad, ready smile for everybody. As a Major, he already had an established Air Force career.

When Del heard that I directed the ambulance pickup and was interested in issues of faith, we met.

"Jon, I'm Del Lockwood, I hear you run the ambulance pick up."

Though he was at first curious about what brand of believer I was, we discovered that for both of us faith formed a meaningful ingredient of life. In the evenings, we would socialize in his room in our upgraded brick barracks. We shared our journey of faith, deepened our friendship, and like all aviators, swapped flying war stories. Because both of us flew as aircraft commanders, we did not have the opportunity to fly together.

On June 10, 1969, Del flew a dangerous airdrop mission into Ben Het. An enemy round hit their plane, and debris sprayed his cheek. He laughed at his discount Purple Heart. No discount needed. The wound, the medal, and Del Lockwood were the real thing. I valued his mentoring of a junior flyboy.

After Caribous, he went to fly C-130s out of Taiwan. It was in that mission that his aircraft was lost in the South China Sea. I was sorry to lose this great friend.

It was a special pleasure to honor Delbert's memory at the fall 2011 reunion of the C-7A Caribou Association in Dallas, Texas, and to have his family present.[20]

Risk and Foolishness

We lived with risk but tried to avoid it where we could.

I flew a night mission from An Khe and was level over heavily wooded terrain, floating in the seeming peace and blackness of night. Then I saw something small and red coming toward me. Shocked, I missed the significance of the red dot. How could anything small be at my altitude. I watched as it went over my left wing as I cruised at 120 knots. Yes, I should immediately have jinked (turned quickly) to avoid it. The glow of a tracer bullet meant there were more rounds that I could not see. Enemy tracers could be either green or red.

Finally, reality hit home. *That was a guy shooting at me. He aimed his machine gun, or AK-47, and squeezed off rounds in front of my aircraft to meet me. At this altitude, the rounds reached their maximum height, thus it looked like they were standing still. Ouch!*

Whoever was shooting was a very good shot and read my aircraft almost perfectly! His accuracy illustrated the risk of a straight course in the presence of the enemy. Other aircraft, closer to the surface, always flew a curving or varied course.

The first USAF Caribou lost in Vietnam (S/N 61-2387) was downed in December 1967 by Vietcong small-arms fire. A single bullet severed a fuel manifold, causing fuel starvation to both engines. Luckily, the pilot crash landed in a rice paddy near Binh Thuy, and all the crew escaped.

We never flew low-level over enemy territory at any speed. A .30 caliber round aimed directly up, topped out at about 3,000 feet. I liked my cruise altitude to be that or above. Our greatest vulnerability to ground fire was when we were close to the ground for takeoff or landing.

One of our guys, deciding he was indestructible at our blazing speeds, thought he could fly low level and get away with it. Over a beach north of Qui Nhon, along the coast, he tried it. Nobody would have known about his foolish attempt, but he overflew enemy soldiers. An NVA stitched him up the middle of the aircraft with an AK-47. One of the soldiers in the aircraft was injured in the leg, and maintenance had a lot of bullet holes to patch for his recklessness.

Reckless behavior did not just happen in the air. One of our pilots, desperate for recreation, hired one of the hootch maids for personal recreation between flights. He also joined others who went into town at night, in the village of Phu Cat, to visit the prostitutes. They knew a route crawling out under the wire, avoiding guards and guard towers.

Dodging bullets was risk enough for most of us.

Pleiku Insomnia

"Do you guys know how to use the 60mm mortar?" the Special Forces Lieutenant asked.

"The what?" I answered, shocked. "Are you kidding? We are Air Force."

"No, I am not kidding. Outside, facing the perimeter, there is a mortar to defend against attack. We all have to be ready if Charlie tries to come across the wire. Come here, I'll show you the basics."

Though Phu Cat would occasionally have a small enemy attack, security was much more fragile at Pleiku. It was closer to the Ho Chi Minh trail, and we could, on occasion, observe rocket holes in the ramp.

We took turns rotating to Pleiku to staff the outpost on the flight line. We bunked in the 7th Special Forces compound on the base: spartan rooms, solid chow-hall food, and the mortar.

"Periodically, the enemy tests our perimeter. The mortar rounds from this locker ignite when the shell hits the firing pin at the bottom of the tube. The round will go 200 to 350 yards, roughly where that clump of dark green bushes is."

In daytime at the flight line, our small, white, sandbagged outpost, a bunker above ground, looked out on the aircraft and loads on the line. Inside, a wrought-iron davenport let a tired loader nap between planes. A refrigerator in the back boasted Stateside sodas. The same rule applied as in the 537th lounge. Treat the cold sodas like gold; use them sparingly.

One of the loaders brought his pet monkey, which explored everything in our outpost and was obviously a great pet. He loved soda pop and would drink it from the can. He owned the place until a dog came by. Terrified, he leapt into the arms of his owner.

There was great variety in our loads. Cows, coaxed into a Caribou, were then restrained with straps. Live sows in wooden crates awaited loading along with chickens in wooden pens. Crated cabbages and vegetables waited with palletized artillery ammunition. On one occasion, neat Vietnamese troops wearing red berets waited for their airlift.

If you heard a racket on the runway, it was the versatile A-1E Skyraider, highly effective but a throwback to World War II technology. In the future, I would serve with the former commander of this unit, Mike Perino.

One privilege of Pleiku was the base exchange. Though smaller than our own at Phu Cat, it had treasures that our own did not stock. I bought a string of pearls for my wife Beverly for our first anniversary.

But sleeping in the compound was another story. I slept all night with an elevated heart rate. *What was that noise? Is that Charlie coming across the wire? Will they sound a siren when he attacks?*

Copilots and a Screaming Dive

My ears popped as our aircraft dropped 2,000 feet, screaming toward planet earth's brown hills and sparse green forest. From 3,500 feet, my copilot Clyde dumped the nose down, down, down.

What in the world is he doing?

I had asked my cohort if he wanted to make the descent to traffic pattern altitude.

Is he bored? I wondered.

Maybe he was longing for his own bird, his Aircraft Commander checkout.

Is he frustrated with me? I was a by-the-book, by-the-rote pilot—probably boring to some.

Going west, 3,500 feet kept us out of rifle and pistol ground fire, but we needed to drop to our pattern altitude for Pleiku.

Once checked out, I invariably flew with competent and helpful copilots. I respected my crew members as valued partners in our mission, first in the Caribou and later in C-118s with a large crew. There was no room for arrogance or one-upmanship. Teamwork best accomplished our fascinating and challenging missions and kept us alive.

At times, having flown with so many copilots, I forgot their names and faces. Now in the Caribou Association, I have met them again and am deeply impressed with their professionalism and offer of friendship. Often, I allowed my copilots to fly the aircraft, honing their skills. I was not an instructor pilot, so I could not change seats or let them make the landing.

At Tra Bong, a small strip with a church and an elephant, Jake, an Army loader, once questioned me privately. "Is your other pilot really a colonel?" He had seen the egg salad on the shoulders of his flight suit.

In the spring of 1969, I had a string of lieutenant colonels who had been flying a desk back in the States. They were getting back in the cockpit for their Vietnam tour; some aviated with me for a week or more. Veterans of the cockpit from years past, they brought years of experience. They respected me, though a young second lieutenant, one whose whole effort was given to the flying mission. They never tried to pull rank.

As a copilot myself, I had groaned to see the book of forms an Aircraft Commander had to complete at the end of a mission. Sorties flown, mechanical condition, enemy fire, mission problems—all had to be recorded. Now, though it took extra time, I loved it as part of my new role.

Though taken on a screaming dive, I could not hold a grudge against Clyde. We did arrive at a lower altitude, though somewhat worse for wear. I remembered my own failures as a copilot. Clyde gave me permission to put his picture with mine on the cover of this book.

CLOUD OF CHOPPERS

Where are the choppers? I puzzled as we landed to the north at Camp Evans. Normally, when we landed, a sea of helicopters filled my view: utilitarian UH-1H Hueys, small bubble-canopy Loaches that looked like toys, and mean, sleek Cobras that bristled with guns. The large pad that once held them, east of the runway, was completely black.

Inquiring of our loader, we heard the sad reality. "A couple of nights ago, Charlie hit us with some mortars. Some of the rounds hit the pad. They all went up in a massive inferno."

"Couldn't you even save some of them?" we questioned.

"Nope," As you saw, they were parked right next to each other."

Were they jammed together to conserve space? The same situation was present on the Pearl Harbor ramps during the Japanese attack on December 7, 1941. The aircraft were parked wingtip to wingtip. Those who do not learn from history are destined to repeat it.

All the wreckage had been cleared, but the massive loss of costly aircraft shocked me.

Our intersection with chopper pilots at runways was the most dangerous part of our operation. They themselves told us that some of the old-school pilots, the brown-shoe boys from the old Army, sometimes turned their radios off in operations, even around the strips. When landing or taking off, we needed to keep choppers under close observation. On occasion, they would drift across the runway unexpectedly, near us or in front of us. It made no difference what the tower said, if there was a tower.

We respected these guys, but especially the Huey and Dustoff medevac crews. On one occasion, at Duc Pho, an Army Dustoff pilot asked if we had heard about a downed aircraft he was searching for. We had no information but saw their passion to rescue, hazarding their own lives.

We heard accounts of some of them descending into small jungle clearings, their rotor blades cutting saplings on the way down. They often airlifted huge loads of wounded. Some mechanics knew how to tweak the Huey engine to get more power. Operating at airports with a cloud of choppers had its challenges. But the dedication of these pilots in heavy combat and the Dustoff crews risking their lives for others, marked them as some of the heroes of the war.

On the Gauges

I don't know what in the world I am doing. The thought came in a VOR approach in pilot training in the T-37 as my instructor labored to teach me the intricacies of an instrument approach. The VOR, or Visual Omni-Range, was a radio aid to navigation on the ground by which a pilot could navigate to an airport.

My slowness in adjusting to this discipline, among others, was what caused my instructor, Kent TeKrony, to periodically holler, "Put your hands in your lap."

Then, flying by the gauges was all new. Approaches in Vietnam were my next classroom. There, only a few fields such as Tan Son Nhut, Ben Hoa and Da Nang had more sophisticated approaches, precision radar, or ILS (instrument landing system). Normally, the best a field would have in poor weather was an NDB (non-directional beacon) on the ground. Combined with an ADF (automatic direction finding) instrument in the airplane, the pilot had a needle that pointed to the station. The simple beacon allowed us to fly an approach to the field in monsoon weather. As a less technical approach aid, the approach plate showed only minimum altitudes at various points in the approach.

But NDB approaches in Vietnam gave me the feel for all instrument approaches because they were straightforward. When the field was socked in, I normally flew out from the beacon at a thirty-degree angle from the final approach course then turned to the final approach track. Crossing the beacon again, I descended to minimums, looking for the field if I broke out of the soup. The whole maneuver was called a teardrop because of its shape.

When I went to fly C-118s out of Clark AB, Philippines, we relied on instrument approaches constantly, especially in Japan and Korea's winter weather. Our minimums of 100 feet above the approach end of the runway and quarter-of-a-mile visibility, kept my heart rate up. Often, I saw the field only at minimums.

But I was not through with the NDB after Vietnam. Hong Kong, one of my favorite destinations, used that approach aid to its Kai Tak Airdrome. Fog, smog, stratus, or rain often complicated visibility. Before the sixty-degree turn to the runway, we had to spot two small checkerboards on a hill, make our sharp turn, drop like a rock, then land. Someone rated the Kai Tak approach the sixth most dangerous airport landing in the world. The hazardous airport and approach has since been replaced by the Hong Kong International Airport on Chek Lap Kok Island.

Though the humble beacon was the simplest of instrument approaches, it was my friend and teacher.

FLUBS AND HUMANITY

"**O**ur landing gear is not down!"

A two-by-four slammed into my fogged brain. The statement came from my copilot when we were on short final for Qui Nhon.

My initial mental response was, *That can't be!* But he was right. What had gone wrong?

Of the normal nine steps on the landing checklist (T.O.-1C-7A-1CL-1), nine are done by the copilot, and one is done by the pilot. Three of the steps are: mixtures—auto rich; propellers— 2250 rpm; gear—down. The only step assigned to the Aircraft Commander is the command, "Gear—down." In response, the copilot lowers the gear handle then both pilot and copilot check that there are three small glowing green lights showing that the gear is, in fact, down. Though the lights failed once in pilot training, they never failed for me in the Caribou.

We had made landings all day, perhaps fifteen, and were tired. Because we had run the landing checklist so many times, we thought we had run it this time.

One danger of routine in flying is mentally being "already there," instead of living in the present. Without thinking of the current steps needed, I had a tendency to think of the things I needed to do on the ground, details of unloading and loading, checking with the agency we were servicing, refueling, and catching lunch if it was close to the middle of the day.

If I had rounded out above the runway and closed the throttles without the landing gear locked down, a warning horn would have sounded. A red light would have illuminated in the landing gear handles. But, until then, getting the gear down depended on the gray matter of the pilots.

My copilot had saved me from landing gear up, almost the ultimate flub in the Bou. It was forgivable, but just barely.

The incident raised darker, more troubling questions. Friends had landed gear up. Others had been part of tragic accidents where human error, flawed judgment, or a broken aircraft intersected. In other tragedies, small oversights or looking the wrong place at the wrong time had spelled great loss.

I remember looking at one of our older pilots after he landed gear up, then smiling. *The fool. Any idiot can avoid landing gear up,* I said to myself. *I am better. I am a hotter, sharper pilot. I could never make that error.*

Of course, we landed safely at Qui Nhon thanks to the alertness of my copilot. But I never forgot my error. It was the reality of humanity.

I stand shoulder to shoulder with all my brothers. I, too, am human and flawed.

FLUBS AND DECISION MAKING

s a transport, I'm like a big, noisy green whale floating around the pattern. An easy target. I've got to shorten this downwind leg to the bare minimum to keep the bad guys from shooting at me.

Downwind was the longest part of the rectangular landing pattern, followed by base and final, landing to the east at Dak Seang where we had once toured the Special Forces bunker. I didn't want the NVA gunners to target me the way they did at Ben Het. But my shortened landing pattern did not have a final approach long enough to get my airspeed down.

Frustrated, I went around for another try.

Recovering from mistakes or miscalculations is a part of flying. Every pilot hates to make a go-around, a confession of failure to everyone on the ground. But it is safe and necessary. You usually have plenty of time to try again and get it right.

The whale again floated around, but my second approach was complicated by an increasing crosswind from the left. The use of wing flaps on landing is a judgment factor. More flaps mean a lower landing speed and a shorter ground roll. But flaps with a crosswind made control more challenging and a smooth wing-low touchdown more difficult.

Faster aircraft used a variety of techniques to handle crosswinds. Some aircraft choose to land in a crab (aircraft angled into the wind) or have landing gear that can be oriented for that type of landing. Some faster aircraft use a kickout landing where the aircraft angles (crabs) into the wind then the pilot kicks out the crab just before touchdown.

Wrestling for control in the crosswind beat me, and again I made a go-around, a second confession of failure. It burned me, but I would rather be safe.

By the third approach I allowed enough of a final approach and a better balance of reduced flaps to touch down on the numbers. I appreciated the gentle uphill in the last half of the landing roll to slow before the ramp.

The decision whether to continue with a questionable landing is critical.

On one occasion, I was too hot on a landing at Ben Het but thought I could get away with it. I made the landing and stopped in plenty of time, but it was not a good or safe landing. I should have gone around.

Throughout my Air Force flying, I had a tendency to land "hot," to carry a little extra airspeed "for the wife and kids."

Life and flying are most wisely encountered with patience, forgiveness, and periodic go-arounds.

WHOSE TURF IS IT?

"Something is on the runway," my copilot commented as we approached the coastal strip.

Peacefully grazing on the grass beside our runway and crossing it to graze the other side, was a group of eight to ten cow-sized animals. Dark brown to almost black in hue, they had large, peaceful eyes. Their flat, crescent-shaped, ribbed horns protruded on either side. Of course, there was no control tower and no base commander to shoo the beasts off his runway. The sight of our bird overhead did not bother them. They didn't even look up.

We had been assigned to land at a small strip along the coast, and aviating there skirted a quilt of coastal villages, wooded mountains, and fishing boats. Or, were those enemy sampans in disguise?

Sometimes coastal towns displayed white idols or shrines on a hilltop, contrasting to the hills and forests. Not much evidence of a war going on until we got to the *New Jersey*.

The massive gray battleship fired broadsides into hot coastal areas of Vietnam. As America's most decorated battleship, it was designed in 1940 and launched in December 1942. Serving in World War II and

Korea, the refurbished model was rolled out in 1968 to support the conflict in Vietnam. The shells from its nine main battery guns were sixteen inches in diameter (406 mm). It was amazing to see the boat rock when the big guns flashed.

The beasts on the runway may have eyed us and thought, "Who do they think they are?" The water buffalo, one of the traditional symbols of Vietnam, symbolizes bravery, happiness and prosperity. Varying from 600 to 1,200 pounds, they are often the most valuable possession of a farmer—almost a member of the family. A mainstay of the economy, they pull plows, carry crops, or carry household children for a ride.

To land without clearing the runway might have meant a quick meal for the villagers, as their meat is preferred over beef. But, we did not want to tangle with them nor they with us.

We made a low pass down the runway at twenty feet, and the cattle decided to amble to quieter grazing a ways off but might return for our takeoff. During our routine unloading the cargo handler said, "Gee, I'm sorry about the water buffalo. They own the place unless you convince them otherwise."

We taxied out for takeoff and saw our friends grazing safely at a distance. They did not challenge us for the runway, delaying their transformation into water buffalo steak.

OPERATION ELEPHANT

"**D**rury, saddle up. You're taking a load to Tra Bong. The forklift is bringing out your load."

If there was ever an earthly version of heaven it was the little strip of Tra Bong. There palm trees, friendly villagers, and a beautiful little church with a white gable roofline greeted us. The village well of large stones stood nearby our strip. But the highlight was the gray elephant if he was there. We always hoped the elephant would be out, the only one we saw at any of our strips.

The dirt runway began after a river and a steep bank. You did not want to land short and wipe off your gear. I touched down beyond the bank and reversed props, raising the cloud of dust normal for a dirt strip.

Climbing down the incline of our ramp, I saw our gray medium-sized elephant was there, giving a welcome flap with his big ears. With short, small white tusks, he looked content, the mascot and hero of the village.

I commented to the Special Forces troop helping with my offload. "We always love to see your elephant. Is it one from this area?"

"Actually, there are two elephants, Bonnie and Clyde, both Asian elephants. They were not native to this area at all. We have been working with this village for over two years, and one of our projects was building a sawmill so the village could be self-sufficient. But the villagers had nothing to pull the logs out of the forest. They said an elephant could do it. We located two elephants at another one of our camps. Then came the job of relocating them to Tra Bong."

"You have got to be kidding" I replied. "How do you relocate elephants?"

"They tied each of them to huge improvised pallets. They went first by C-130 to Chu Lai about a year ago then were brought to Tra Bong via Marine CH-53. The elephants survived the transport and have been working at the sawmill since then. Though you see one here at the airstrip, the other is hard at work."

He added, "They say the C-130 flight was a disaster for the crew. The elephants were given tranquilizers before the flight, to calm them, which caused gas that the crew barely survived. Some said the air was blue or green, and you could cut it with a knife. The gaseous emissions shimmered like heat waves, and were said to be of eye-watering quality."[21]

CHU LAI AND THE CORPS

Why use a runway to land? When landing to the south at Chu Lai, because we were a short takeoff–and-landing bird, we could swoop down on the overrun of 500 to 700 feet. We could turn off at the ramp without ever going down the runway. Tower tolerated our shortcut, but like typical military, didn't appreciate our disrespect for procedures. It saved time, and we flaunted what hot short field jocks we were.

What made Chu Lai more interesting was it being a United States Marine Corps base. No mistaking. A settlement did not exist there before a Marine landing on May 12, 1965. The name Chu Lai was not marked on local maps. Though it was fifty-six miles south of Da Nang, it helped take some pressure off the dense traffic operations of that field.

On the base, I loved seeing the array of Marine and Navy fighter bombers and knew that they were hard working aircraft. We saw A-4 Skyhawks and bulbous A-6 Intruders. I heard that one of the A-4s, with high intakes and no working landing gear, attempted landing on a strip of foam. But emerging at the end of the foam at the same speed, he jammed the throttle forward, lifted off again, and bailed out over the water. There was a gutsy pilot.

One time, landing to the north, two of us Caribous ended up roughly the same place at the same time. Neither of us had seen the other until relatively close. We landed first, and after we did, I waved to the pilots (as in, "Sorry about that!"). Later I learned he thought I gave him the three-fingered salute. Whoops!

On occasion, when we were at the strip at lunch time, we would go to the Marine Officer's Mess. Even in Vietnam, the corps was pretty much spit and polish away from combat in the field. Unfortunately, it was not a friendly atmosphere, though I had just served them by bringing in their supplies.

I doubt that elitism is helpful in a combat environment. Officer Training School tried to breed elitism. I found I needed to lose that attitude in favor of teamwork.

But Marines were their own breed, and Air Force pilots were less than welcome in their officer's mess, even in our flight suits.

It might have changed their perspective had they known we were some of the transports that brought their fallen brothers off the battle field at Dong Ha in their final journey. But they did not know that, and we did not volunteer the information.

We just choked down humble pie along with lunch.

Touches of Home

"Gunfighter Corral." Though I originally knew nothing of the reason for the name of the Air Force compound at DaNang, I loved being there. It was the closest we came to Stateside conditions with a theater: American-style food, and decent transient quarters. And everything was Air Force. We weren't there often but reveled in the benefits when we were.

The name revived the image of an Old West gunfight. I learned it referred to air victories of the 366th Tactical Fighter Wing based there. Moving to Da Nang in October 1966 with the new F-4C, the wing began to register MIG kills at a rapid rate. Their success earned the nickname "Gunfighters" and a presidential unit citation for shooting down eleven enemy aircraft in a six-week period.

On one stop at the corral, I traded war stories with Dave, a pilot training friend, quiet but determined. He earned a Silver Star, the decoration one notch lower than the Medal of Honor, flying a lowly C-47 Gooney Bird. We sat in one of the restaurants and caught up on our journey and what we knew of other pilot training graduates in our class.

We grieved a fellow classmate who had lost his life flying an A-37 Dragonfly light attack aircraft. It was the glorified version of the T-37 we flew in training.

Another large base with good food options was Cam Ranh Bay. The pavilion at Cam Ranh was not only frequented by crews, but also by troops in transit, so the lines were long.

As at An Khe, I fumed, *Dang. Why do there have to be so many of them?* They had time to wait out the line, but we didn't. Though desperate for its goodies—a variety in our mundane existence—usually the best we could do was run in and see if we could get an ice cream or hot dog by the time our bird was ready. When our cargo was loaded, we had to be gone.

Military use of Cam Ranh dated to 1905 when the Russian fleet staged there before a battle with the Japanese, which it lost. The Japanese took control in 1941 and launched their invasion of Malaysia and Singapore. The United States arrived at Cam Ranh in 1964 and created two concrete runways. Military operations for all three services eventually brought 40,000 military and 20,000 civilian employees.

Later, flying the C-118 hospital mission, I often based at Cam Ranh, airlifting patients for care throughout the Pacific theatre. I stayed on the east side of the base with good food, decent quarters, and outdoor movies. Because other crews passed through the busy base, I often saw others I knew.

A refreshing break—Da Nang and Camh Ranh were touches of home.

LIFE BLOOD

"You've got a fuel leak inboard on the right wing."

The flight engineer's breathless statement rocked me out of post-takeoff euphoria. His normal crosscheck of everything after takeoff had caught the leak.

"Let me take a look," I answered. I could not see the right wing from my left seat cockpit position. "Level us and take us toward Qui Nhon," I said to Glenn, my copilot.

I climbed down from my left seat and peered out one of the oval windows on the right side. Inboard, near the fuselage, was a stream of mist indicating a fuel leak. A fuel leak from a fuel cell was rare. More dangerous was a fuel leak in an engine.

Mission over.

"Tower, I'm doing a one-eighty return to the field. We've got a fuel leak."

Fuel is the life blood of engines.

In my first flight in an Aeronca Champ, after takeoff I glanced at the fisheye gas gauge only to see E—empty, no fuel. Horrified, I returned to the hangar only to hear, "It always says empty."

They had not bothered to tell me that.

"You check the fuel by removing the cap of the fuel tank in front and waggling your fingers in the fuel tank to see if it's full," he continued. From then on, I practiced the finger waggle to be sure the bird had been refueled.

Fueling the Caribou was normally done at a larger field by a professional crew. But when we had to refuel our own aircraft, it meant climbing up on the wing via the ladder in the cockpit. Acutely aware of the danger of slipping and falling, perhaps because of spilled fuel, I worked slowly and deliberately. No matter how careful I was, I almost always got fuel on myself.

The danger of fuel contamination spooked us. The indication on the fuel truck might or might not be accurate. Also, a soldier new at his job might get it wrong.

On one occasion when an engine had surging RPM, we landed at Da Nang to have it checked out. No fuel contamination was found. Next day we flew with no problems, and no repeat of the fluctuating RPM.

Fuel contamination might lead to both engines failing at once and a forced landing in a rice paddy, forest, water, wherever you were. I took the threat seriously.

FRIENDLY FIRE

"**I**s that an artillery fire base down there? Why isn't it on the map? Why don't they tell us about these? Do you think he's shooting? Which direction?"

Flying in Vietnam, what you didn't know and couldn't find out, could kill you. The NVA and the Vietcong were not the only dangers.

We all knew that in most of the country, you could be blown out of the sky by a friendly firebase and an artillery mission you knew nothing about. Artillery firebases were built to provide artillery fire for combat missions in the field. In a middle pocket of my flight suit, I carried a little book with the frequencies not only of the ALCEs at various bases, but also the frequency of artillery units throughout Vietnam.

We were shown a classic picture of pieces of a Caribou falling out of the sky. In August 1967, aircraft number 62-4161 had flown in front of a 155mm howitzer. It highlighted the desperate need for coordination between the services. Not an easy ideal to accomplish.

Usually, the call to a firebase went something like this: "Song Be Arty, Song Be Arty, this is Soul Four-Four-Six about to fly south to north

235

through your AO (area of operations). Do you have any fire missions? Over."

Because their first responsibility was not radio communications, you might not get them. But if you did, they might answer, "Soul, no fire missions going at present, good day, Sir." Or they might answer "Soul, suggest fly five clicks east due to fire missions. Good day."

If I was not able to reach them, I could either watch for artillery smoke or give their site a wide berth. But locating firebases was far from an exact science. Bases were moved and new bases built. I got my list from other guys, had my hands full with flying, and couldn't constantly be searching for new ones.

In combat situations, we used an FM (called "Fox Mike") radio to talk with ground forces. When asked for a frequency, a noted American showman often came into play.

"Yellow tail, can you give me the freq for Song Be Arty?"

We might answer "Freq is Jack Benny's age plus point six five." The theory was that the NVA knew nothing about American culture.

A more dangerous friendly fire hazard was Arc Light strikes, B-52 raids of pattern bombing. I tell more about that danger in another chapter.

We dreaded getting hit by lethal friendly fire.

FLIGHT MECHANIC

Don's broad smile welcomed me to the bird some mornings when he was in my crew. He was a flight mechanic, and his great work ethic meant he was already hard at work inspecting everything.

In the Caribou missions in Vietnam, we were usually a crew of three: Aircraft Commander, Copilot, and Flight Mechanic or Flight Mech (FM), unless we had a Flight Examiner or Instructor with us. One of the special contributions of the Flight Mech was his expertise in strapping down loads. They were all top notch at this. We used broad, white, synthetic cargo straps that could be ratcheted tight. That system worked for most loads of light to moderate weight. For heavier loads, the Mechs used chains that could be tightened.

In World War II, aerial engineers flew on a wide variety of bombers and transports, and crew chiefs flew on C-46s and C-47s. At some point, they started calling the flying crew chiefs Flight Mechanics. They were not only experts at strapping cargo, but good at switchology, fixing a broken aircraft on the road. A Flight Mech could take training and testing to upgrade to Flight Engineer, who, on larger aircraft, had a panel of gauges and controls. Through the '60s and '70s, Flight Mechs were used on a wide variety of aircraft.

In flight, the Caribou FM could occupy the jump seat between pilot and copilot. To assist ground operations, he could climb the ladder in the cockpit and stick his head out of the top of the cockpit to assist in clearance from other aircraft and fixed obstacles.

For the information of those who do not fly, the weight and balance of an aircraft for flight is critical. The aircraft must be loaded within limits and at the stations in the cargo compartment prescribed in the manuals. Crew members who do not pay attention to weight and balance die quickly. One thing you knew about a Caribou was that your load did not exceed limits, except in emergencies, and would never shift an inch. Once the Flight Mech tightened down a load it did not move.

A testimony to this fact was found in the Bou we lost at Camp Evans in October 1968. Tragically all lives were lost. The aircraft ended up upside down in a swamp, but we heard that when examined, despite the collision and crashing inverted, the load was still strapped in place.

It was my honor to complete the affairs for Don, the Flight Mech on the flight, after the accident.

Don, your load never moved. Well done!

You Can't Miss
from Fifty Feet

The most amazing story of a Caribou flight engineer is that of Frank Godek when the enemy besieged Dak Seang. Caribou emergency resupply airdrops were being made into the base, some of them hair-raising. The commander of the Pleiku ALCE told Frank that DakSeang had burned out its desperately needed four-deuce mortars (4.2 inches in diameter). He asked Frank, "Can you assure me that we can get two, four-deuce mortars and ammunition into the base?"

"If we load the mortars in the middle pallet and put the ammunition on the pallets on either side, we can get them into the camp," Frank answered.

When his aircraft commander, Lieutenant Lewallen, arrived at the airplane and learned the situation, he asked Frank what he thought about that load and getting it into the camp.

"We can't miss from 50 feet," Frank replied. The A/C agreed.

The copilot chimed in: "Don't I have anything to say about this?"

Their ship was the fourth in a five-ship formation, the other aircraft dropping from 300 feet. When they approached the drop zone and began to descend, the forward air controller hollered, "Pull up, you're getting too low." Two Caribous had already been lost to heavy automatic weapons ground fire.

The copilot called out fifty-foot increments in the descent on the radar altimeter. At fifty feet over the zone, Lewallen hollered, "Green light." Away went the mortars and ammunition.

Back at Pleiku, the ALCE Commander told Frank, "The mortars are already in place and firing."

"The camp sends their thanks for a job well done."

"You can't miss from fifty feet," Frank answered.

In those few days, Frank flew a total of eight airdrops at Dak Seang, both day and night. Frank was familiar with the camp since on another trip to the base he had been hosted for lunch in the underground Special Forces bunker

Pat Hanavan's comment on this incident in Caribou Airlines, Volume Four: "In retrospect, this mission should have earned the crew the Silver Star, but that did not happen."[22]

LEPROSARIUM

When Dave stopped the jeep, a short woman's big smile and friendly wave welcomed us to her village as if we were small children. She had stubs for fingers. "Me, Mary," she said.

Outside of Qui Nhon we had stopped to visit the Quy Hoa Leprosarium, or leper colony, established by a doctor priest in 1932. As the road connecting the colony with the main city of Qui Nhon was fit only for goats, with ruts and sand dunes, it was good we went by jeep. From where we visited with Mary, we could see through the trees the stark white sand beach of the South China Sea. Troops went there for in-country R & R, a welcome respite from combat.

The leprosarium was home to over 1,000 Vietnamese afflicted with Hansen's Disease who had no place else to go. The disease had ravaged their hands and feet since there was no cure at that time.

Fourteen Roman Catholic nuns—seven French and seven Vietnamese of the order of Franciscan Missionaire de Marie—were the guiding forces behind the facility. Though decades of fighting surrounded the 175-acre facility, it operated continuously. The non-native sisters left during Japanese occupation in World War II, but the Vietnamese sisters remained.

Fourteen main buildings and a village of 230 two-room houses accommodated patients and their families. In addition, there was a school, a church, and a four-wing hospital. With no paid employees and little money for upkeep, all the work to maintain the hospital was done by the patients themselves. Those who were too sick to leave their beds were cared for by others.

The patients made bricks, erected buildings, cooked food, cleaned rooms, kept the grounds, laundered, and cared for orphans left by parents who had died of the disease. They caught fish in their own man-made pond and grew fruits and vegetables.

The South Vietnamese government paid about fifteen cents per patient per day. The rest of the funds came through private donation.

My mind reeled at the physical and social agony and disconnection from what we know as a normal way of life. Yet there seemed to be a cohesive sense of order and even tranquility. *How could one live without the use of fingers, hands, arms and legs?* I puzzled.

Even today, the village has many descendants of the original residents, some of whom work in a small clothing factory or as crab fishermen. Other compassionate people minister to the needs of the patients, often children of the former residents. Seniors stay in their homes until death.

Thankfully, a cure is now available, a multi-drug therapy (MDT), widely distributed in the 1990s.

Surprisingly, I found the residents to be like Mary—shy, quite friendly, and at peace.[23]

FROM CARIBOU TO C-118

"**D**rury, your assignment came in," the ops officer said, handing me a white envelope.

My next assignment. Always a big deal for a guy in the military. Toward the end of my year at Phu Cat, I submitted my preferences for my next aircraft assignment. Hoping to be assigned back in the States, I asked for a Stateside assignment, perhaps enabling Bev to finish college.

That didn't happen, but I was fascinated to learn I would fly C-118s out of Clark Air Base in the Philippines. The C-118 was the military version of the 1950s Douglas DC-6, a dependable piston engine prop plane.

I would aviate with the 6485th Operations Squadron, which emerged from World War II with tons of history, originally flying C-47s. Its hospital mission throughout Asia shuttled patients to needed medical facilities. Initially, many of our patients came from Vietnam. The unit took great pride in its mission, and our seven birds had a stylish red half-arrow on their side.

A popular airliner of the 1950s just before the jet era, the DC-6 notably flew with United Airlines. The rock-solid R-2800 Pratt and Whitney engine powered the historic P-47 Thunderbolt and F-4U Corsair of World War II fame. It was the most dependable reciprocating engine I ever experienced. I never suffered an engine failure.

I began looking for the red arrow C-118s on the ramp at bases. When I found one, I ran over like a kid at Christmas, met the crew, and walked through the aircraft. Though big compared to the Bou, I could see myself in this bird.

One bummer was that I could no longer start the engines myself. That was the flight engineer's job. I would miss counting blades, engaging the spark plugs, feeding in prime, and nursing the starting cough of the engines.

I would be able to bring Beverly on the assignment, so we would pack up our things in Lubbock, Texas, and now make our home at Clark Air Base. We would ship our goods there along with a newly-purchased blue 1967 Ford Mustang.

One high point of flying C-118s was the opportunity to take a C-118 that belonged to the base to Hong Kong, Kai Tak airdrome. At the time, Kai Tak, with its checkerboard approach, was one of the most challenging airports in the world.

Through scheduling with Base Operations, the bird would be filled with folks who wanted an outing to Hong Kong. I would put Beverly in the passenger compartment, seats facing backward as for all C-118s. Then we were off to Hong Kong, one of the great places on the planet.

Though the 6485th was somewhat ingrown, the C-118s and Clark would allow me to tour much of Asia, a job I loved.

AFTER VIETNAM

Forgotten Conflict

Like most Vietnam veterans, we were pressured by society to forget about Vietnam when we returned home. The conflict was our fault. At the very least, the conflict had been controversial and divisive. You didn't wear your uniform, read about it, or talk about it. Nobody wanted to hear.

I had invested four years flying as a pilot in two different aircraft. One year at Phu Cat, Vietnam then three more years flying into and out of Vietnam from Clark Air Base in the Philippines.

When I returned, family members gave me a warm welcome, but the reception of the public was nonexistent.

Though others experienced a great divergence of opinion on the war, we who flew the Caribou knew why we were fighting. We fought to give the South Vietnamese people a choice of freedom. I felt that mistakes in the prosecution of the war wasted some of the great sacrifice. Eventually our commitment waned, and the country fell to the north.

Like many others, though proud of my personal role, my unit, and my mission, when we returned, we had none of the victory celebrations such as VE day and VJ day in World War II.

But, because of the Gulf War and other reminders, the nation realized that the fighting man was not to be blamed for the decisions of politicians.

Unfortunately, the dishonor to those who served in Vietnam has had a tragic legacy. Many of the men, despised for their service, became a lost generation, damaged by the experience. For some it meant disease, despair, or an early death. Many became homeless.

But some came alongside. When I registered for my VA identity card, the black lady who took my application made a point of especially assisting Vietnam vets. Thanks.

After I returned, for perhaps ten years, I read nothing on Vietnam. Then, the nation began to discover the power in healing the memory of that forgotten conflict. I have visited the Vietnam Wall in Washington, DC three times. I have located and photographed names of men I knew who perished.

A wall was built in Sacramento, California, which I visited. A public parade remembered our service and sacrifice.

I read *Chickenhawk*, an incredible book about First Cavalry chopper pilots in Vietnam just before my era, flying where I was flying. The powerful book began to remind me of what we experienced.

One product of the new awareness is the phrase heard often: "Thank you for your service. Welcome home! Glad you made it back."

I was able to share it with a combat infantryman this morning.

The Caribou Association

In my black suit, I waited in the lobby of a funeral home to perform a service for a friend. Before the service, a man of medium height with a handlebar moustache approached me.

"Do you know who I am?" he asked.

"I have no idea," I answered.

"I'm Charlie Tost," he replied.

As part of the 537th TAS in Vietnam, as I have related, Charlie was the instigator of a lot of fun during our flying year 1968–1969. He was the reason a number of us grew the stache during our year.

You could have knocked me over. I had contact with only one former Caribou pilot in my area, and he was not one I had flown with.

"Do you know that we have formed an association of former Caribou flyers?" Charlie asked.

I knew nothing about it. He gave me contact information for the C-7A Caribou Association, and I attended my first reunion at Midland-Odessa Texas in October 2004. There I discovered a great group of guys associated with the Caribou, not only pilots but also Flight Mechs, maintenance, and administrative personnel.

At the reunion, I discovered that many significant things were being done to remember what we accomplished and to honor those who died flying the Caribou. Increasingly, memorial benches have been placed in significant locations, honoring the Caribou guys who died in Vietnam.

I also learned that though some had thought about making memorial patches of the units, none had been made, so I began investigating how it could be done. I found the graphics required would take $60 to make one patch. I began searching for manufacturers who could make a high-quality product and reduce the price by buying one hundred patches at a time. I have since supplied patches of all the primary flying units to the association, at exact cost.[25]

A painstaking part of the process was researching patch designs because several designs were available for some patches. I usually chose the most common design, but, on occasion, I chose the most attractive design to my eye. I purchased the best reference books available on Air Force patches in different eras.

I still have one association friend who says, "You made the wrong patch for my squadron!" Having seen multiple designs for the same unit, I had picked the nicest one according to my eye.

The most difficult research was the patch for the 483rd TAW (Tactical Airlift Wing), but finally we found a plaque that gave the needed detail.

Asked to be one of the chaplains, it is an honor to serve. We chaplains not only give invocations and assist in dedications, but we are also available to assist any of the members, their families, or the Association.

I cannot conclude appreciation of the Caribou Association without mention of Pat Hanavan's monumental five volumes of *Caribou Airlines* (available from Amazon.com). They are a comprehensive history of USAF C-7A Caribou operations in Vietnam. They are an invaluable reference to each era of the airplane in Vietnam operations.

EPILOGUE

My C-118 assignment at Clark Air Base, Philippines, 1969–1972, brought me to the historic 6485th Operations Squadron. Beginning with WW II Gooney Birds, the squadron transitioned to the C-54, then the C-118—the dependable DC-6, all with the same hospital mission throughout Asia. They seldom received new pilots and felt some resistance to the two of us who arrived from Caribous in Vietnam. Their medical mission proved fascinating, and we flew with a dedicated medical crew.

Beverly and I lived off base initially then moved into on base housing where orchids grew in our front yard.

I was offered a regular commission. Because I felt drawn to ministry, I refused the commission, though I considered it a great honor.

On discharge, Beverly and I and our infant son trekked to Dallas from the San Francisco Bay Area. Transiting Phoenix in 110 degrees, we melted without air conditioning. After a stay in Odessa, Texas, with Bev's family, I registered in Dallas for Bible training.

We purchased a home surrounded by native pecan trees in a scenic, older neighborhood. I went to school on the GI Bill. Funds were tight, but we washed our clothes in a laundromat and survived. An uncle had given me a coin collection, and little by little, we sold the coins. At Dallas Federal Savings I microfilmed records then served as an industrial chaplain in a food plant.

Chandra, our second child, had lungs. When I got off the elevator at Baylor Hospital after her birth, I could hear my red-headed singer all over the floor. Later, she recorded children's albums.

We found a church desperate for anyone to lend a hand. We sponsored youth and taught Bible classes, and I drove a Sunday School bus to poor neighborhoods.

On graduation, though I had thoughts of ministering to the military, I went to a small rural church in Snohomish, Washington.

We loved raising our young family in the logging town with a view of the Cascade Mountains. Our family grew with the addition of two more daughters. Heating the uninsulated 1920s parsonage in zero degrees proved a challenge. The river turned to chunks of ice, and I hurried to the Port of Everett for deadhead logs to split for firewood. I tied the logs to the top of my Pinto and loved the cedar fragrance that filled the house when they were burned.

Pastoring proved stressful, but again we learned and survived. We returned to Castro Valley, California, to my home church—Redwood Chapel. For thirty-two years we fulfilled our dreams, mine of teaching, pastoring, and mentoring writers. Bev managed a credit union, retired, then skillfully led a Women's mnistry.

In 2010, I published *Lord, I Feel So Small*, explaining my discovery of answers to many struggles I faced in life.[25]

At retirement, the congregation rewarded us with a trip to the Holy Land.

We moved to Vancouver, Washington, where we enjoy retired life and frequent contact with grandchildren. I have continued to fly, mostly Cessnas out of Pearson Field, but I love tailwheels.

Memories of flying the Caribou, now revived by the Caribou Association, recall warm comradeship.

End Notes

1. http://www.yeapeople.com/Age3/avhist/Jenny.html.

2. Of the two classes of which I was a part, 68-D, 68-E, roughly 30 percent of the men were unable to finish pilot training successfully.

3. Col. Pat Hanavan, USAF, Ret., *Caribou Airlines, A History of USAF C-7A Caribou Operations in Vietnam, Vol. II Tet Offensive, 1968* (Create Space, 2013), pp. 267–268.

4. http://www.c-7acaribou.com/history/images/Caribou_Brochure_Web.pdf.

5. Summary history of the 483rd compiled by Robert Blaylock, www.c-7acaribou.com.

6. *Caribou Airlines, Vol. II*, p. 238–239; *C-7A Caribou Association Newsletter,* Vol.25, Issue 1, March 2014, p.11.

7. *Caribou Airlines, Vol. II*, p. 238–239.

8. *C-7A Caribou Association Newsletter*, Vol. 27, Issue 2, April 2016, p.22; *Caribou Airlines, Vol. II*, p. 247–248.

9. *C-7A Caribou Association Newsletter*, Vol. 27, Issue 2, April 2016, p.16.

10. *C-7A Caribou Association Newsletter*, Vol. 25, Issue 2, December 2014, p.10.

11. Official accident summary http://www.vhfcn.org/midair.html; *Caribou Airlines, Vol II*, p.260–261.

12. *C-7A Caribou Association Newsletter*, Vol 26, Issue 1, March 2015, p. 7.

13. A nice account of Worley's life is found at *stevenlossad.blogspot.com/2013/07*.

14. *C-7A Caribou Association Newsletter*, Vol. 26, Issue 2, November 2015, p. 27.

15. *Caribou Airlines, Vol. II*, p.356; *Caribou Airlines, Vol. III*, p. 222–223.

16. *Caribou Airlines, Vol. II*, p.256; *C-7A Association Newsletter* Vol. 23, Issue 2, November 2012, p. 26.

17. *Caribou Airlines, Vol. III*, pp. 208–209; *C-7A Caribou Association Newsletter*, Vol. 24, Issue 2, Dec. 2013, p. 19.

18. *Caribou Airlines, Vol. III*, pp. 197–198; *C-7A Caribou Association Newsletter*, Vol. 23, Issue 2, November 2012, pp. 26–27.

19. *C-7A Caribou Association Newsletter*, Vol. 25, Issue 1, March 2014, p.10; *Caribou Airlines, Vol. II*, pp. 336–337.

20. *C-7A Caribou Association Newsletter*, Vol. 24, Issue 1, May 2013, p.21; *Caribou Airlines, Vol. III*, p. 203.

21. *C-7A Caribou Association Newsletter,* Vol. 27, Issue 3, November 2016, p.21; *Caribou Airlines, Vol. II,* p.334, Movie Operation Dumbo Drop, 1995, was made about the incident. https://en.wikipedia.org/wiki/Operation_Dumbo_Drop.

22. *Caribou Airlines, Vol. III,* p.220.

23. https://www.afar.com/places/queens-beach-and-quy-hoa-leper-colony-tp-quy-nhon.

24. *C-7A Caribou Association Newsletter,* Vol. 1, Issue 21, Jan. 2005, p. 12.

25. Published Dec. 22, 2010, Winepress, now printed by *Deep River Books.* The book is available on Amazon.com.